MW01621181

CONVERSATIONS

AT THE UNITED NATIONS

CONVERSATIONS
AT THE UNITED NATIONS

**AN INSIDE LOOK AT THE PERMANENT MISSIONS,
UN ADMINISTRATION,
AND NONGOVERNMENTAL ORGANIZATIONS**

Thomas V. McConnon

Legwork Team Publishing
New York

Legwork Team Publishing
New York
www.legworkteam.com

ISBN: 978-1-935905-82-0 (hc)

Disclaimer: The information provided in this book is based on a compilation of monthly conversational meetings between Rotary International and distinguished UN ambassadors, international representatives, and special guests. It is intended to provide the reader with "behind the scenes" insights and a clearer understanding of the United Nations and its worldwide role.

Conversations and situations have been transcribed from actual Rotary/UN meetings, and the author and the book's contributors have taken every care in representing conversational details. Information, opinions, and references to individuals named herein are believed to be accurate and all contributor submissions are used by permission.

All Internet address links appearing in this book were verified when the manuscript was submitted for publishing. However, neither author nor publisher has control of subsequent changes made by Internet website administrators.

The views and opinions expressed in this publication are solely those of the author, Rotary International guest speakers and listed contributors, and do not necessarily reflect or represent views or opinions of Legwork Team Publishing or its staff. The publisher, its staff, and agents have done their best to ensure full informational integrity throughout, but make no guarantees whatsoever regarding the accuracy, comprehensiveness, utility of the work, suitability, or validity of information or philosophies stated, quoted, or implied herein, and will not be liable for any content errors, omissions, or inaccuracies. However, please inform us if any inaccuracies are noted so they may be corrected in future editions.

First Edition 02/13/2018
Printed in the United States of America
This book is printed on acid-free paper

To Barney and Josef

The publication of this book was made possible by a grant from the CSR (Corporate Social Responsibility) account of Thomas Refrigeration and Air Conditioning Service Company, Inc., Garden City Park, NY
(A Service for the New York Real Estate Manager.)

All of Mr. McConnon's royalties for this book are being assigned to the *Foundation of the Rotary Club of New York* and *The Rotary Foundation* in equal proportion. Both are highly-rated, tax-exempt 501(c) (3) organizations under the Internal Revenue Code.

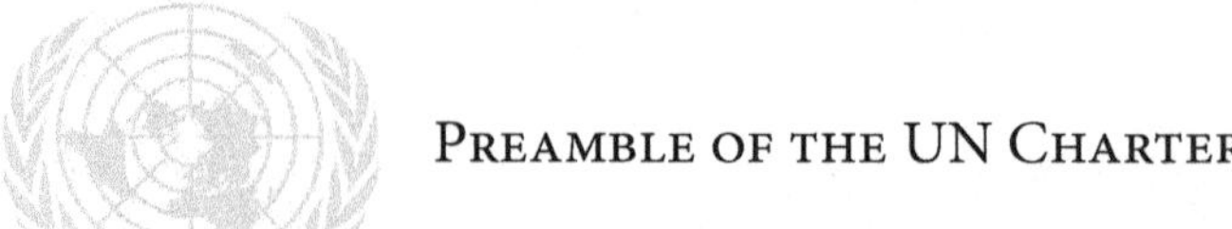

Preamble of the UN Charter

WE THE PEOPLES OF THE UNITED NATIONS

determined

to save succeeding generations from the scourge of war, which twice in our lifetime has brought untold sorrow to mankind, and

to reaffirm faith in fundamental human rights, in the dignity and worth of the human person, in the equal rights of men and women and of nations large and small, and

to establish conditions under which justice and respect for the obligations arising from treaties and other sources of international law can be maintained, and

to promote social progress and better standards of life in larger freedom,

and for these ends

to practice tolerance and live together in peace with one another as good neighbors, and

to unite our strength to maintain international peace and security, and

to ensure, by the acceptance of principles and the institution of methods,that armed force shall not be used, save in the common interest, and

to employ international machinery for the promotion of the economic and social advancement of all peoples,

have resolved to combine our efforts to accomplish these aims.

Accordingly, our respective Governments, through representatives assembled in the city of San Francisco, who have exhibited their full powers found to be in good and due form, have agreed to the present Charter of the United Nations and do hereby establish an international organization to be known as the United Nations.

CONTENTS

CONTENTS

CONTENTS

FOREWORD

My friend Tom McConnon's book, ***Conversations at the United Nations,*** gives a unique insight about Rotary's relationship with the United Nations. He reports about many conversations between Rotarians and leaders who work with the United Nations. These include Diplomats, United Nations Administrators, Nongovernmental (NGO) Leaders, and Rotary Leaders.

The best kept secret about Rotary is that Rotarians are active in peacemaking activities around the world for many years. With Rotary's 1.2 million members in 215 countries and territories, there are usually Rotarians on both sides of any conflict between different countries. Rotarians are friends, even if their countries are enemies. Rotarians also have good relationships with the leaders of their countries. This provides a great platform for peacemaking.

The reason that most people are not aware of Rotary's contributions to peacemaking is that Rotarians are modest people, who do not like to take credit for their achievements. Tom has been a Rotarian for many years and his book tells the story that has been hidden for so many years.

The book also has a chapter about Rotary's role in the founding of the United Nations. Forty-nine Rotarians helped draft the United Nations Charter in San Francisco, and many delegates from around the world were Rotarians. At the organization conference of the United Nations held in San Francisco in 1945, the United States delegation invited Rotary International to appoint consultants. Rotarians served in this capacity with resulting influence on the humane aspects of the Charter. Rotarians at San Francisco helped rewrite the Preamble ("We the peoples ..." rather than "We the states ..."). Secretary of State Edward R. Stettinius, Jr. wrote:

> *The invitation to Rotary International to participate in the United Nations Conference as consultant to the United States delegation was not merely a gesture of goodwill and respect toward a great organization. It was a simple recognition of the practical part Rotary's members have*

> *played and will continue to play in the development of understanding among nations. The representatives of Rotary were needed at San Francisco, and as you well know, they made a considerable contribution to the Charter itself, and particularly to the framing of provisions for the Economic and Social Council.*

Josef Klee, PhD has written a section in the book about the relationship between the United Nations and the Holy See (the Vatican State). Dr. Klee is a Rotarian and a Retired United Nations Executive. In his retirement, Dr. Klee serves as a Member of the Holy See Delegation to the United Nations.

Conversations at the United Nations *An Inside Look at the Permanent Missions, UN Administrators, and Nongovernmental Organizations* is a very interesting book for those with a passion for peacemaking and Rotary's relationship with the United Nations. You will find it very interesting to read.

Matts Ingemanson
Chair, Founding Member
Grassroots Peacemaking

District Governor 2013-2014
Rotary International District 7230
New York & Bermuda

Founding Member
Chair 2004-2006
RGHF (Rotary Global History Fellowship); a Rotary Fellowship authorized by the Board of Directors of Rotary International

PREFACE

Since 2002, Rotarians and their like-minded guests have been invited to attend the NY Rotary monthly International Breakfast Meetings that have been normally scheduled on the third Wednesday of every month and held at the Church Center, opposite the UN at 777 UN Plaza, 44th St. and First Ave. Previously, we met at the German House located at 871 United Nations Plaza, 49th St. and First Ave. These meetings have provided an opportunity for Rotarians to stay updated on United Nation programs and to exchange views on related topics with UN officials, NGOs, and representatives of Member States. There were usually no meetings in September when the General Assembly met. Reservations are required to attend the meetings and can be made at: ny.rotary@verizon.net. The monthly meetings were originally coordinated and moderated by NY Rotarian Dr. Josef Klee, Deputy Director of the United Nations (Retired) and the late Sylvan "Barney" Barnet, Alternate Rotary International Liaison to the UN. Our newsletter editor was yours truly, Past Assistant District Governor for Manhattan and Riverdale, Thomas V. McConnon.

ACKNOWLEDGMENTS

I would like to acknowledge the dedicated efforts of Janet Yudewitz of Legwork Team Publishing and its attentive editorial staff. I extend my gratitude to them and their team of design and technical professionals for transforming my manuscript into the book you hold in your hands.

INTRODUCTION

The first announcement to establish a "United Nations Organization" to help prevent future global aggression was made by FDR in January, 1942, just a few weeks after Pearl Harbor was attacked. At its founding, the UN had 51 Member States—primarily those countries united to defeat Germany and Japan. Today, there are nearly 200 members. The buildings in New York were completed just a few years before I was born in 1952, and were designed by Brazilian and Swiss architects. The new UN Headquarters was greeted with much fanfare and was the "Pride and Joy" of New York City.

Growing up in Queens, NY in the 1950s and 1960s, I thought that the United Nations always existed. Driving into Manhattan, (aka "The City") with my dad, or looking towards the city from my uncle's bar and grill on Queens Boulevard in Sunnyside, Queens, there was that iconic, beautiful, turquois glass, modern building of the United Nations Headquarters—one of the most notable buildings in the world.

It was not until years later that I found out how fragile the concept, and actual creation of the United Nations organization was, even though at the time, it was considered "man's last chance for peace." The UN was not always there, it was the replacement for the ineffective League of Nations in Switzerland.

My father was a sergeant in the United States Marines during World War II, so that makes me a "baby boomer." The one thing that our generation shares is that our fathers served four-years fighting in WWII. However, while our parents' generation was less likely to talk about their service, they knew first-hand how destructive and painful war is.

Both of my parents, and their parents, and their grandparents also grew up in Brooklyn. My parents raised me and my four siblings in Queens, New York, in a two-family house. (We were two or three miles, as the crow flies, from the neighborhood where President Donald Trump grew up.) My siblings, my friends, and classmates, learned how agonizing war was from them. Furthermore, we thought we could expect another war. We had air-raid drills during those days where we had to retreat to our basements when the testing of the sirens sounded.

I remember taking several grammar school field trips to the United Nations, and touring the futuristic *General Assembly* that we all frequently watched on television, especially when the United States and The Soviet Union were at odds. Yet, my fondest memory of the UN was when my sister and I, and tens of thousands of all the NY area Catholic School students in their respective uniforms, lined the highway from JFK airport in Queens to the United Nations in Manhattan, to welcome and a get a glimpse of Pope Paul VI. That was the first time any Pope ever visited the United States. But he came to address the "world" at the United Nations in 1965, and not necessarily to visit New York, or Washington. At that time, the name of the JFK airport had just been changed from Idlewild Airport, in honor of recently assassinated President John F. Kennedy, for whom Pope Paul VI offered condolences in his address to the United Nations. Two other Popes since then have addressed the General Assembly as well, years later. A few sentences from Pope Paul VI's address provide the indication that something important was happening:

> *Was not this the very end for which the United Nations came into existence: to be against war and for peace? Listen to the clear words of a great man who is no longer with us, John Kennedy, who proclaimed four years ago: 'Mankind must put an end to war, or war will put an end to mankind.' There is no need for a long talk to proclaim the main purpose of your Institution. It is enough to recall that the blood of millions, countless unheard-of sufferings, useless massacres, and frightening ruins have sanctioned the agreement that unites you with an oath that ought to change the future history of the world: never again war, never again war! It is peace, peace that has to guide the destiny of the nations of all mankind.*

In the mid-1970s, when I was a student at New York University, I remember being invited to a party at Tudor City, the multibuilding, high-rise, residential apartment complex across the street from the United Nations. I recall seeing the beautiful UN complex from the thirtieth floor of Tudor City, and how it really was the *World's Center*. Nevertheless, I still did not know that much about the people who spent their days working there on a daily basis, and what they were all working on.

I first learned about Rotary during my Peace Corps Volunteer Service in the early 1980s. The Peace Corps offered me to start-up a refrigeration and air conditioning training program in St. Vincent, West Indies. It was to be designed to teach the "young men of the West Indies to repair the equipment that the region already had." However, when I arrived at the technical college, I found that my 700 sq. ft. classroom was empty. There were no desks, no books, and no equipment. Fortunately, the dean of the college informed me that the local Rotary Club had arranged funding. I knew nothing at all about Rotary up to that point in my life.

While the PolioPlus Program had TRF (The Rotary Foundation) commitment of more than $1.2 billion, it also had the Matching Grants Program. Since this program's founding in 1965, it has funded more than 40,000 projects for a total of more over $500 million. Very often, Peace Corps Volunteers' projects were also supported by The Rotary Foundation, and the volunteer's hometown Rotary Club matched the grant. In my case, my project was awarded $125,000 in 1981. The Rotary Foundation Matching Grant, and Canadian Rotarians provided the required $125,000 additional matching funds.

Within several weeks, the local Rotarians of St. Vincent told me that The Rotary Club of Toronto, Canada confirmed that they sent a container load of tools, books, desks, and even a small pickup truck to use. Within two months, my classroom was properly supplied, and more than thirty young men were learning the skills necessary to repair refrigeration and air conditioning equipment, providing them with a marketable skill.

I have to acknowledge, if not for The Rotary Foundation, my students would have wasted months waiting for the USAID (The United States Agency for International Development) grant, which eventually did come, and the students would not have been trained as thoroughly. However, most importantly, meeting with, and working with the West Indian and Canadian Rotarians, I knew that I would need to join Rotary once I completed my service and relocated back to New York. So, I did, and that was thirty-five years ago!

A few years later, when I was a thirtysomething President of the Hicksville-Jericho Rotary Club in 1988, several of the wiser past presidents of the club recommended that I go to this newly established Rotary/United Nations event at UN Headquarters. They knew I had an interest in the United Nations as a Returned Peace Corps Volunteer, and that I was committed to international poverty reduction projects through Rotary, especially our worldwide flagship program PolioPlus Program that was just recently established. The mission of the program was to eradicate Polio from our planet, and the UN was not yet a partner in this program. They also knew that my loving wife, Noemi, whom I met while I was a Peace Corps Volunteer (and was somehow fortunate enough to convince to return with me to New York) also worked with the World Health Organization of the United Nations.

It was at this first Rotary/United Nations Meeting I attended at the UN, where I first met Sylvan Barnet or "Barney" as he is cordially known. Barney had arranged for about fifty Rotarians to meet in one of the smaller conference rooms with three scheduled speakers: an ambassador, an administrator of the UN, and an NGO director that worked with the UN. It was about a three-hour presentation, and then we all had a late lunch, drinks, and lots of laughs at the UN Dining room. Since those small annual meetings, Barney's Annual Rotary/United Nations event grew to bring in more than 1,500 Rotarians with all the top brass of Rotary International attending the sold-out event every year.

Fast-forward fifteen years to 2002. I decided to transfer to a New York City Rotary Club because my company was now much more Manhattan oriented by that time, and for me to attend a Long Island Rotary Club, I would have to lose the day of work. So, I applied to the "Grandfather" of Rotary Clubs: the legendary Rotary Club of New York. This club had 250 members and was created in 1909, with a very well-established foundation.

Once again, there I had the pleasure to meet up with Barney, and he remembered me from our meeting so many years earlier. He welcomed me to my new club, and invited me to the recently-established RCNY monthly International Breakfast Meeting that was held at the German Mission, across the street from UN Headquarters. It was there that I first met Josef Klee. "Joe" was a recently retired assistant Secretary-General of Personnel of the United Nations. Needless to say, Joe knew everybody at the UN, and he would schedule the speakers for our informal and friendly monthly gatherings. We also enjoyed the best croissants this side of the "Pond" as Barney would say. Joe and his lovely and very supportive wife, Uda, lived just across the street from the United Nations, they moderated the meetings with grace and charm, and there was never a dull minute.

In fact, the meetings were terrific. An informal, friendly discussion with UN personnel and Rotarians (primarily business-owners and professionals) discussing our mutual objectives, and how Rotarians and the UN could partner in achieving these goals. The meetings were officially scheduled from 8:30 a.m. to 10:00 a.m., but most meetings usually ended around 12:00 p.m. because for another hour or two, many informal conversations and planning sessions continued. We still hold these meetings as of the printing of this book.

For decades, many New Yorkers complained that the UN diplomats did not pay their parking tickets, or that Manhattan traffic came to a standstill when the US President, or the Pope came to address the General Assembly. Some members from the United States Congress want to stop funding the UN because of some of the UN's policies. Yet, it must be said, it is now more than seventy years since FDR and Churchill announced the plan to establish the United Nations, and the world has not had a global conflict since the UN's creation. It is my hope that this book, ***Conversations at the United Nations***, will help the "Peoples of the United Nations" to maybe get a better understanding of how the UN has helped to prevent the "Scourge of War."

One last word: many thanks to my loving wife, Noemi, who for more than fifteen years, would make sure that I was up at 4:30 a.m. in order for me to make it to the city by 8:00 a.m., and she would still make me the best cup of coffee, even at that wicked hour of the morning! And, also, I would like to thank my dear friend, Sheila Washington, who always made the meetings ever more interesting, travelling in from Brooklyn, who would write up a review of the conversations of those meetings I was unable to attend, which are also included in this book.

Tom McConnon
Commack, NY
April, 2017

ROTARY'S ROLE IN THE FORMATION OF THE UNITED NATIONS

The Rotary Club of New York, as well as many other Rotary Clubs, played an essential role in building support during the formative years of The United Nations, and also in selecting New York City for UN Permanent Headquarters. As such, more than sixty-five years later, Rotary International still maintains the highest consultative status with the United Nations of any nongovernmental organization. In this capacity, Rotary International and the United Nations has built a strong and productive partnership in achieving the Millennium Development Goals of 2000, including the global eradication of Polio, cultural exchanges, literacy, education, water/sanitation projects, and promotion of peace conferences around the world.

In the late 1940s, Rotary International was one of the largest international organizations in the world. There were more than 6,800 clubs, in more than eighty-one countries. More importantly, Rotary was already working on projects around the world to diminish the causes of war and aggression. In fact, during a 1943 Rotary Conference, held in London, the outline for the development of UNESCO (United Nations Educational, Scientific and Cultural Organization) was established in 1946, and Rotarians helped write its constitution. Additionally, many of the delegates at the San Francisco Conference that were representing their respective governments, were also members of their own Rotary Clubs and utilized their clubs to develop support for the soon to be established UN (United Nations Organization).

Formation of the United Nations

In August 1941, during the Atlantic Conference off the coast of Newfoundland, President Roosevelt and British Prime Minister Winston Churchill issued a joint pronouncement that an effective international organization would be needed to replace the struggling League of Nations, which was unable to prevent the outbreak of the Second World War. There, too, the Four Freedoms were promulgated as fundamental freedoms humans "everywhere in the world" ought to enjoy: Freedom of speech and expression, Freedom of religion, Freedom from want, and Freedom from fear.

In October 1943, at the Moscow Conference, the "Big Three" and China (referenced now as the "Big Four") formed a Four Power Alliance pledged to commence the creation of a post-victory, international, military force—an organization to maintain peace and quickly curtail any future aggression. The Moscow Declaration stated, "The necessity of establishing at the earliest practicable date, a general international organization based on the principle of sovereign equality of all peace-loving states … for the maintenance of international peace and security."

During August 21-October 7, 1944 at Dumbarton Oaks, an estate in Washington, D.C., the "Big Four" met with the main objective of creating an organization that would maintain international peace and security by peaceful means whenever possible, use economic sanctions and force if necessary; and promote security by encouraging economic and social cooperation among nations. While the foundations were laid out, some details on voting procedure had to be decided at a later time.

In February, 1945 at the Yalta (Crimea) Conference, the provisional government of France was also invited to take a leadership role at the San Francisco Conference along with the "Big Four." In addition, forty-six other countries that waged war against the Axis Nations were also invited to participate at that conference, which was known formally as the "United Nations Conference on International Organization." Their mission was to create the charter for the United Nations basically along the guidelines of those proposed during the informal conversations at

Dumbarton Oaks.

On April 12, 1945, two weeks before the San Francisco Conference was to meet, President Roosevelt died. Exhausted and ill, he was resting at Warm Springs, Georgia when he suddenly complained of a terrible headache. Two hours later, he was pronounced dead of a stroke. Roosevelt was succeeded by Vice President Harry S. Truman, who vowed to continue with the formation of the United Nations Organization.

April 25-June 6, 1945—At the San Francisco Conference, 49 of the 800 delegates and advisers were active Rotarians. Some of the notable Rotarians that attended the conference were:

- Thomas J. Davis, Past President of Rotary International (1941-42) and unsuccessful Republican candidate for the US Senate.
- Luther Hodges, Past President of the Rotary Club of New York (1945-46). Luther also went on to become governor of North Carolina, Commerce Secretary for President Kennedy (1960-63), and President of Rotary International in 1968.
- Gabriel L. Dennis, the Secretary of State of Liberia was a signer of the Charter for Liberia.
- Jan Christen Smuts, the Prime Minister of South Africa from 1919-1924 and from 1939-1948.
- Carlos Romulo of the Philippines was also a signer for the Philippines. He served as Resident Commissioner of the Philippines to the United States Congress from 1944-1946, President of the Forth Session of the General Assembly (1949-1950), and was the Philippines' Secretary of Foreign Affairs from 1950-1984.
- Jan Masaryk, Foreign Minister of Czechoslovakia from 1940-1948.

As a result, it was decided at the conference that the causes of aggression and war, such as poverty, ignorance, and lack of human rights, would have to be ameliorated as well. As a consequence, the UN Charter was designed to help achieve these goals much more than originally planned at the Dumbarton Oaks Conference. Rotarians contributed to the drafting of the United Nations Charter, its Preamble, and the Articles on the ECOSOC (Economic and Social Council) and the NGOs

(Nongovernmental Organizations).

On October 24, 1945, the UN Charter was ratified, the United Nations came into existence, and Rotary helped overcome the United States isolationist sentiment. The UN leaders knew that the American public, and the American political leaders had to fully support the newly created organization. Without full United States support, the soon-to-be created United Nations Organization would be powerless, as had been Woodrow Wilson's discredited League of Nations. With this in mind, the US Department of State commenced a public relations campaign to build support for the proposed organization and partnered with a number of civic and religious organizations, including Rotary Clubs, to build up this support.

On October 9, 1942, the Rotary Club of New York hosted the "United Nations Luncheon" and Sir Gerald Campbell the well-known special assistant to the British Ambassador, addressed 600 members and guests at the Hotel Commodore on E. 42nd St. in New York City. He informed the Rotarians that unity and organization were gradually being achieved by the United Nations. Twenty-one trade and consular officials of the United Nations also attended the luncheon.

On April 16, 1943, Ray O. Wyland, President of the Rotary Club of New York, simulcast its annual "Pan-American Day Luncheon" with the keynote speaker, Undersecretary of State Sumner Welles. The Secretary traced the development of the United States relations with the other Central and South American republics. Attacking the tariffs of 1921, 1922, and 1930, he stated that this slow strangulation of international trade was one of the chief causes of the "world crisis." He asserted that other Western Hemisphere republics "will never forget the dislocations caused in the economic life of many of them by the successive tariff increases in the United States."

On June 27, 1944, Col. C. V. Jenkins, a Past President of the Rotary Club of New York, led the campaign to change the name of Sixth Avenue in New York City to "Avenue of the Americas"—The Gateway to the Americas. The purpose of the name change was to "help make real the dream of a unified Western Hemisphere Community of Nations." Plans where submitted to install flags of the Latin American Consulates and their countries along the avenue.

On August 18, 1944, on his way to London, the President of Rotary International, Richard H. Wells addressed the Rotary Club of New York and vowed to reestablish Rotary Clubs in the Axis countries within five years after the war. At this meeting, he stated that the Nazis had "Run Rotary out of Paris," but Rotary President Wells vowed to reestablish nearly 500 European Rotary Clubs disbanded by the war.

On April 13, 1945—Nelson Rockefeller, Assistant Secretary of State, was the keynote speaker at the annual "Pan-American Day Luncheon" of the Rotary Club of New York. His speech, in front of more than 500 Rotarians, was also simulcast by radio to the Western Hemisphere. Rockefeller stated that, "No nation, large or small can solve all its problems alone. Yet united, we face the possibility of great productivity, prosperity and peace if we work together. That is the purpose of civilization." His speech was broadcast throughout the Western Hemisphere including translations in Spanish and Portuguese. Rockefeller asked that the world's nations affirm their recognition of responsibilities to the world effort, and be pulling for a new workable "international security organization."

In May 1945, Secretary of State, Edward R. Stettinius Jr. invited Rotary International to send one representative and one alternate to the San Francisco Conference to act as consultants to the American delegation. Forty-one other NGOs (Nongovernmental Organizations) were also invited to send a delegate and alternate.

In September of 1945, the NBC Radio Network scheduled seven hours of programs to celebrate "United Nations Week." Secretary of State, George C. Marshall launched the week of broadcasts. Rotary International President, Leo E. Golden, gave a half hour presentation asking all civic-minded businessmen and professionals to support the United Nations. Other speakers included poet and author of the UN Preamble, Archibald MacLeish, and Secretary John Foster Dulles.

United Nations Committee Votes that the new International Organization Should Be Located in the United States and New York City is an Interim Site

On December 15, 1946, at the London Conference after heated discussion and debate, the United Nations committee selected Westchester County of New York and Fairfield County of Connecticut as the general area for the "Permanent Site" for the United Nations Headquarters. New York City was chosen as the location for the "Interim Headquarters" until the exact "Permanent Site" could be located and constructed. The Chairman of the UNO (United Nations Organization) Headquarters Committee, Dr. Eduardo Zuleta Angel of Columbia, stated that "New York is a city where every race and every nation of the world is represented, where the different peoples of the world are molded in a common society."

The reasons that the United States was chosen by the UN Preparatory Commission were:

- Europe was no longer the world's political or economic center.
- Unlike the League of Nations, if the new UNO is located in the United States, it would ensure United States participation.
- Europe could break out in war again.
- United States government maintained neutrality and abstained from voting on location.
- Russians were strongly in favor of the United States as the location.
- Geneva (site of recently completed League of Nations compound) was not an option because "Swiss neutrality" would demand that any Security Council decision to use military force had to be held outside of Swiss borders.

At the time, it was originally discussed to create a self-contained campus that was somewhere between two square miles and forty square miles in size. On March 26, 1946, the UN Security Council opened its first session at the "Interim Location" at Hunter College's Gymnasium in the Bronx. A few weeks later, Secretary-General Trygve Lie also selected the New York City building from the 1938 World's Fair site at Flushing Meadows for the temporary meeting hall of the General Assembly, the Secretariat, and the Security Council.

The other bodies and commission would meet at the Sperry Gyroscope plant at Lake Success in Nassau County. The New York City building at Flushing Meadows was rent-free and reduced rent for the Sperry plant was paid by the War Assets Corporation. New York Officials hoped that the Flushing Meadows location would be considered for the Permanent Site of the UN Headquarters. Robert Moses, the New York State Public Works Commisioner was authorized to spend $1.2 million to improve the Flushing Meadows site, and Secretary-General Lie signed a three-year lease for the Sperry plant for the General Assembly. Robert Moses, made available 1,612 apartments in Parkway Village, Queens, and Peter Cooper Village at the average cost of $25 per room.

In December 1946, Rotary Clubs organized to host 250 employees and delegates of the United Nations to spend a three-day Christmas Holiday in private homes in Binghamton, Endicott, and Johnson City in Upstate, New York. A chartered train took the guests to their destination. In that same month, 175 New York Rotarians visited the Temporary General Assembly Building at Flushing Meadows, Queens. This is the current site of the US Tennis Open, and the building is now a public ice rink. A few weeks later, sixty members of the Philadelphia Rotary Club were also welcomed at the Lake Success Building.

However, on December 10, 1946, Westchester and Fairfield Counties eventually rejected the UN Headquarters located in their counties, and UNO (United Nations Organization) needed to seek a new location. Protest from increasing numbers of Westchester and Fairfield County citizens caused the Selection Committee to reconsider locating in Westchester and Fairfield Counties.

Also, the Lake Success and Flushing temporary sites offered by New York City were too far from the city and unattractive. As such, President Truman offered the San Francisco Presidio, the beautiful military base with parklike grounds overlooking the Golden Gate Bridge rent-free. However, the Europeans thought this was too far from Europe.

Philadelphia offered the attractive Belmont-Roxborough site. It was on the eastern coast of the United States, and was considered attractive to most members of the site location committee. However, on Friday night, December 6, 1946, at the midnight hour before Philadelphia was to be voted on as the Permanent Site, Secretary-General Lie, Robert Moses, and Mayor O'Dwyer called Nelson Rockefeller, Assistant Secretary of State. They asked him to arrange for his father to finance the purchase of a six-block area of slaughter houses and run-down buildings on the East Side of Manhattan known as Turtle Bay for $8.5 million. They thought it was "worth a try" since the Rockefeller family had generously donated the library to the League of Nations and the family was very supportive of the new international organization. Then amazingly, on December 15, 1945, New York City was voted to be site for Permanent World Headquarters

On March 26, 1947, Mr. Trygve Lie, the first Secretary-General received an $8,500,000 gift from John D. Rockefeller III to purchase the land at the Turtle Bay section of New York City where the UN headquarters is now located. New York Rotarian Robert Moses was instrumental in helping to locate the UN World Headquarters in New York.

Rotary Starts the Ambassadorial Scholarship Program

In September 1946, President Truman at the National Commission of Education, Scientific, and Cultural Cooperation in Washington, asked the attendees to assist the United Nations. In his speech, the President stated, "It is understanding that gives us the ability to have peace. When we understand the other fellow's viewpoint, and he understands ours, we can sit down, and if there are differences, we can work them out." As a consequence, at the June, 1947 Rotary International Convention in Atlantic City, N.J., Rotary International expanded its one-year-old program and awarded fifty-five additional "Ambassadorial Scholarships" to college graduates from fifteen countries to study for a full year in another country of their choice.

On June 9, 1948, Rotary International and the Carnegie Endowment for International Peace partnered to donate $12,000 to bring forty students from UN "Member States" to intern at United Nations Headquarters. The interns stayed at Adelphi College located near Lake Success, and had lunch at the United Nations Cafeteria. Up to this time, the UN had several interns only from the United States, but this grant also welcomes students from foreign countries with opportunity to work at the UN.

In June of 1949, The Rotary Club of New York hosted the 40th Rotary International Convention at Madison Square Garden. This was the largest Rotary International Convention with more than 15,000 attendees and its theme was to support the United Nations and UNICEF (United Nations International Children's Emergency Fund).

Mr. Trygve Lie, first Secretary-General of the United Nations and the convention's Keynote Speaker, addressed the Rotary International. The full text of his address appears in the Ambassadors' section, which follows. New York City's Mayor O'Dwyer welcomed the delegates of fifty countries. He stated that it was fitting that the United Nations was in New York because "the city is an example of how people of all nations and races can live together peacefully."

Also at the convention was British actress Ms. Madeleine Carroll, the highest-paid woman film star at the time. She also challenged Rotarians to take up the cause since the United Nations had up to this time failed to realize its goal. The rehabilitation of hungry and sick children of war-torn Europe still needed to be solved. Ms. Carroll, who was the only woman speaker at the convention, received a standing ovation in tribute. Ms. Carroll's address can also be read in the Ambassadors' section, which follows.

A letter by President Harry Truman was also read by the Secretary of the Navy at the Rotary Convention. The President stated:

> *I believe it is equally important, that to the world's orderly progress, that business leaders of all nations also have much closer ties than in the past. Certainly, one of the greatest influences for bringing that about should be Rotary International. I am sure that it will be, for Rotary has always been at the forefront of any great movement for improving the welfare of people everywhere.*

At this convention, Rotary voted to spend $750,000 during the next three years to promote better understanding and friendlier relations among the peoples of several nations. Additionally, part of the funding was to be used to send speakers to various countries to explain the workings of the United Nations and promote international unity.

In June, 1959, The Rotary Club of New York hosted the 50th Annual Rotary Convention and once again, the theme was "Promoting Support for the United Nations."

On June 12, 1959, Dag Hammarskjold, the second Secretary-General of the United Nations, addressed the closing session of the 50th Rotary International Convention in Madison Square Garden, New York City. He called for government and business to help the "less fortunate countries." Mr. Hammarskjold's address is included in its entirety in the Ambassadors' section, which follows.

THE AMBASSADORS OF THE PERMANENT MISSIONS

A Permanent Representative, also known as "UN Ambassador," is the head of a Member State's diplomatic mission to the United Nations. While the most high-profile representatives are those assigned to the UN Headquarters in New York, Member States also appoint Permanent Representatives to the other UN offices in Geneva, Vienna, and Nairobi. UNESCO, UNHCR, and UNICEF as well as others, also appoint "Goodwill Ambassadors" that are very often celebrities to help bring publicity to their organization but they have little policy control.

Mr. Trygve Lie, First Secretary-General of the United Nations, Addresses Rotary International's 40th Convention at Madison Square Garden in New York City, June 1949

Mr. Trygve Lie was raised in Kristiania, Norway., He earned a law degree from the University of Kristiania, Oslo. After the German invasion of Norway in April 1940, he was appointed foreign minister of the Norwegian government-in-exile in London. He was a Norwegian politician, labor leader, and diplomat before being nominated to be the first Secretary-General of the United Nations by the Soviet Union from 1946 to 1952. He would not be reappointed to a second term largely because of the Soviet Union's resentment of his support of UN military intervention in the Korean War. He died in 1968.

"The United Nations, Bridge to Peace"

Four years ago this month, the 26th of June, 1945, the Charter of the United Nations was signed in solemn ceremony at San Francisco. This was a great achievement for the cause of peace—one of the greatest in human history. It was rightly a moment of exaltation for men and women of goodwill throughout the world. The four years since then have brought many, many disappointments.

The great majority of people all over the world have not lost their belief in the United Nations as the best way. But they are worried, worried deeply about the future. They believe in the United Nations Charter but they wonder how it is going to be made to work.

If they live in the Western world, they worry about the "veto" blocking the will of the majority. If they live in Eastern Europe, they worry about mechanical majorities "riding roughshod" over the minorities. If they live in Asia or Africa, they worry about "how much help or how much hindrance" the UN will prove to be in their struggle towards peace.

In 1945, most people thought of the United Nations primarily as a security organization which would crack down like a policeman with a club, or when needed, a gun, whenever an aggressor raised his head. In its first four years, the United Nations has not been able to get the Great Powers to agree on what kind of military forces, and how many should be placed at the disposal of the Security Council. As a result, today the international policeman is walking around trying to keep nations from fighting each other, not only without a gun, but without even a club to help him to do his job.

As for the nations themselves, the plan was for them to start cutting down on their armaments as soon as the United Nations forces were operating and to set up control systems which would safeguard everybody from the use of weapons of mass destruction such as atomic bombs and biological warfare.

This plan is just as far from being realized today as it was four years ago. There are no United Nations forces. The world is spending more for armaments than ever before in peacetime. No agreement has been reached on the control of atomic energy. The majority of nations supports the United

States plan, which the Soviet Union and its allies have refused to accept. The minority has advanced alternative proposals, which the majority has flatly rejected. As for germ warfare, rockets, and the like, they have not even been discussed.

All this makes a discouraging picture. Through it all and underneath it all, of course, the poison of the East/West conflict of interest and ideology is constantly at work—the main cause of the trouble.

If this were the whole story of the United Nations, we would be right to despair for the future of the human race. For if this were the whole story, then we would be forced to the conclusion that the effort to prevent a third world war is doomed to failure. We all know what would happen to civilization if a third world war is permitted to occur. There could be no victor, no vanquished, only universal destruction and disaster.

The fact is, of course, that this is not the whole story of the United Nations by any means—far from it.

As I drove in to New York City from Lake Success, Long Island the other day, I was thinking how I might be able to make this plain. I thought of our temporary headquarters in the Sperry Gyroscope Plant out there, a plant which was built to supply war contracts. We have about half the building and the Sperry Company still operates in the other half. The United Nations has about 3,000 employees and so does Sperry. There are two big parking lots, and each of them has about as many cars as the other.

I thought that this symbolizes the contradictions of the world we have been living in quite well since the San Francisco Conference. However, while it dramatizes the situation of the United Nations, it does not explain it. Then, at the end of my journey from Lake Success to Manhattan, I found what I was looking for. It is a place I visit frequently, and it is just a few blocks from this hall where Rotary International is meeting. It is the site of the permanent headquarters of the United Nations.

There, in the vast excavation between 42nd and 48th Streets next to the East River, the steel skeleton of the building that will house the United Nations for generations to come has been anchored in foundations of solid rock and already rises above the surrounding buildings. Only the girders are there now. It does not look much like the artist's drawing of the finished building that is displayed in the public lobby at Lake Success.

I ask you to think of this steel skeleton as the United Nations and the

Specialized Agencies as they exist today. The foundation of solid rock is the United Nations Charter. It is upon this foundation and around these ribs of steel that we are engaged in building, stone by stone, and floor by floor, what will ultimately become the completed structure of a peaceful world society.

The buildings over on the East River will be completed in 1951. Six years is not a long time for a building project of this magnitude. Building a peaceful world society will take a good deal longer. We have to think in terms of decades, not years. If we keep at the job all the time and never falter we ought to be able to get quite a lot done in the next 20 years, and a great deal more in 50 years. If we can keep on building a peaceful world on a United Nations basis all that time without a war, then permanent peace will really be within our grasp.

This may seem a very long and a very slow process to a country that is still as young in spirit and as impatient to achieve good results as is the United States. But even present-day Americans and their ancestors took over 300 years to build the United States into what it is today.

In that scale of time, 50 years is a very short time in which to accomplish so great a result as the prevention and abolition of war. I think it can be done, and I am not an optimist. People who come from northern countries where there are many mountains and the living is hard, are more inclined to realism than to optimism. They have to be. I have already given you a fairly complete summary of the things that the United Nations has not yet been able to do. Against these must be placed the things the United Nations has done and is now doing.

The United Nations has not yet been able to enforce peace, but it has been able to persuade nations to keep the peace and to bring them back to the conference table when they threatened to fight each other, or even after they started fighting.

The last war left the whole world in ferment and disorder. This was bound to be the case after so universal and destructive a calamity. There have been literally hundreds of important disputes between nations since the United Nations was founded. There have been at least a dozen serious crises. There has also been the continuing crisis of the so-called "cold war."

The differences, serious and otherwise, that caused all these crises existed before there was a United Nations and could not be removed by magic just because the Organization was established. What the United Nations could do, and what the United Nations has done, is to get these conflicts settled peacefully, or else to keep them within peaceful bounds—and if fighting started—to get the fighting stopped.

In Palestine, a new nation has been born without a major war in a truly historical achievement that has behind it not only 30 but 2,000 years of accumulated sorrows and bitterness, oppression, hatred, cruelty, and countless previous failures to arrive at a settlement.

In the great subcontinent of India, where 400,000,000 people live—the worst kind of warfare—religious war has been averted by a cease-fire agreement reached by India and Pakistan under United Nations auspices.

In Indonesia, where 70,000,000 people live, the United Nations has been working for two years to bring about a just and peaceful solution of the struggle between the Dutch and the Indonesians seeking independence. There have been many ups and downs in this effort, just as there were in Palestine, but the influence of the United Nations keeps reasserting itself and seems destined to prevail.

I could give you many other examples of United Nations work for peace. We have, in fact, been called in to virtually every trouble spot in the world. There is a United Nations Commission in Korea. There is a United Nations Committee on the border of Greece. Three years ago, the United Nations was appealed to when "big power" troops overstayed their leave in Iran, in Syria, and in Lebanon. In all cases, the troops were withdrawn after the Security Council had discussed the matter.

Most important, and most dangerous of all, was the deadlock over Berlin, which was brought to the Security Council last fall as a threat to the peace. This was a complaint by three of the great powers against a fourth.

Many people thought this crisis would lead to the breakup of the United Nations and even to the ultimate disaster of a third world war. Neither of these things happened and one of the main reasons why they did not happen was that the United Nations set in motion forces of mediation and conciliation, which at first did not succeed, but which persisted and eventually prevailed.

The world should never forget that it was because of discussions by United Nations delegates in United Nations headquarters that agreement was reached to lift the Berlin blockades and to set the Council of Foreign

Ministers to work once more upon the peace treaties.

In all this, the United Nations has not had a single gun at its disposal. A dozen of its representatives, including Count Folke Bernadotte, have died at their posts—literally soldiers of peace whose only weapon was the moral force that could be mobilized by the United Nations. In every instance, this moral force has, in the long run, prevailed.

I call to your attention, furthermore, that a large share of this work for peace has been accomplished by the Security Council, which to hear some people tell it, has been completely paralyzed by the "veto." In the face of the "cold war," there has been plenty of trouble with the unanimity rule, but I submit that "paralyzed" is not the right word to apply to this record in the prevention of war.

Rotarians, I know, are especially well qualified by the nature and purposes of their own organization to understand the roles of the General Assembly, the Economic and Social Council, and the whole vast network of commissions and specialized agencies in the building of a peaceful world.

The General Assembly is written down by some people because, as they say it cannot make laws. It makes, in general, only recommendations. But the General Assembly, in four short years, has already shown itself to be perhaps the most powerful mobilizer of public opinion the world has ever seen, and public opinion is the maker of all law, whether it be local law, national law, or international law. An example of what I mean is the Universal Declaration of Human Rights. This Declaration is not a law, but it is just as important as if it were, and it may be as significant for world history as the Declaration of Independence was for the United States. That wasn't a law either, but it was responsible for quite a lot of progress in the world!

The Universal Declaration of Human Rights is the first attempt in history to write such a declaration for the whole world, not just for a single country. It took two years to complete it. Already it is being appealed to all over the world by people who believe they have just grievances. It has been cited, even in the United States, in a case before the Supreme Court. I predict that this Declaration is going to mean as much as any law, because it sets a standard for governments to live up to, and if they don't live up to the standard, they are going to hear from the people. In fact, they have, in many places, already begun to hear from them.

Another interesting aspect of the General Assembly that has become apparent in the past four years is the chance it gives to the small countries to get their grievances aired and to exert influence in the settlement of issues. In this respect, the Assembly is like the traditional "town meeting" in the United States. The man who has a little shop down the street gets a chance to be heard on a basis of equality with the man who controls the bank. And that is good not only for the small countries, but for the whole world. It is good because too much power in the hands of anyone is bad for everyone. Americans, with their constitutional system of checks and balances, understand that very well.

In world affairs, the General Assembly gives the small countries a chance to act as checks and balances upon the power of the great countries and also upon the power conflicts of the great countries. That is the most important of all, because it is these power conflicts that in the past have always led sooner or later to wars. Applying the brakes early enough to these conflicts is one of the main reasons for the results achieved by the United Nations in keeping the peace. The General Assembly is doing this all the time when it is in session.

Often this function is overlooked because the process of applying the brakes is usually covered over by a long and apparently fruitless debate; you have all heard the taunts about the United Nations being just a debating society. Of one thing I am sure; no war of importance will ever be started while the General Assembly is in session. An aggressor just could not get away with it.

The United Nations is working against war now or next year. It is also working against war 20 or 50 years from now. It is doing this work against future wars primarily through its economic and social machinery and through its work for dependent peoples. This work is being carried out on an immense scale. In four short years, a dozen specialized agencies and as many commissions have been organized to deal with problems of labor, investment, health, food, agriculture, trade, education, aviation, children, refugees, human rights, technical assistance, economic development, freedom of information, and many, many, related fields of activity. Thousands upon thousands of businessmen and scientists and economists and experts of all kinds have been mobilized for this work, and they are working every day in every part of the world.

Rotary International has given valuable help in this work on many occasions and in many ways. In this connection, I wish specially to thank Rotarians for their active support of the International Children's Emergency Fund and the United Nations Appeal for Children. They will need your support more than ever this year, and I know they will get it.

There can be no substitute for the universal approach of the United Nations. Regional action in the economic and social field can be of immense value, provided that this action is carried out within a universal framework. Regional action in the political field can help to redress the balance of forces at work in the world, provided that it is in conformity with, and subordinate to, the universal Charter of the United Nations.

There is only one way, however, by which to prevent a third world war in the long run. The only way is to bring into the United Nations, and to keep within the United Nations, all the nations of the world and to make the United Nations work on a universal basis.

I believe that the four years between June, 1945, and June, 1949, have shown under very difficult circumstances that the United Nations can be made to work, that this must be done, and that the peoples of the world are going to see to it that it shall be done!

Before closing, Mr. President, I want, again, to thank personally all members of Rotary International and all national groups of Rotarians for their understanding of the United Nations and the help, which they have given in its work. The sympathy and cooperation of Rotarians everywhere has always been an inspiration, and I am happy that the United Nations and Rotary International are so closely associated.

Thank you all very much.

Ms. Madeleine Carroll, the First "Goodwill Ambassador" for UNICEF Addresses Rotary International's 40th Convention at Madison Square Garden in New York City, June 1949

Ms. Madeleine Carroll, the first defacto "Goodwill Ambassador" for UNICEF, although it was not officially known by that title in 1949. She starred in the Alfred Hitchcock classics The 39 Steps *and* Secret Agent, *and more than three dozen other movies and was the highest paid actress in the world at the time. During World War II, her sister was killed in a German air raid on London, and Ms. Carroll went back to England, where she did war relief work.*

She was born in 1906, near Birmingham, England and graduated from Birmingham University with a BA degree with honors in French. She got roles in several British movies, beginning with three films in 1928. She became an American citizen and in the United States appeared in Hollywood films including: The Case Against Mrs. Ames *(1936),* The General Died at Dawn *(1936),* Lloyd's of London *(1936),* On the Avenue *(1937),* The Prisoner of Zenda *(1937),* It's All Yours *(1937),* Blockade *(1938),* Cafe Society *(1939),* Honeymoon in Bali *(1939),* My Son, My Son, *(1940),* North West Mounted Police *(1940)* Virginia *(1941),* One Night in Lisbon, *(1941),* Bahama Passage *(1942), and* My Favorite Blonde *(1942).* Relief Work in World War II. *She died in 1987.*

"The World Unites For Children"

Ladies and Gentlemen: First I'd like to say how deeply I appreciate the honor you have done me in asking me to speak this morning at your first plenary session. I am told that I am to be the only woman speaker of the week, which makes my responsibility a very heavy one.

Whatever happens I must uphold the honor of my sex, and if I should fail in my responsibility towards the children in whose behalf I am speaking today, I would indeed be an unhappy woman. However, I am somehow not too afraid, for even though this is such an enormous place, and you are so many, there is coming from you to me such a good warm feeling of kindliness, that even though I did not know I was among Rotarians, I think I could guess it. And it is because you stand for kindliness and good neighborliness that I want to speak to you; just as one speaks to good neighbors and friends, and not as an alleged actress talking to the public.

Just for the next few minutes I want you to forget you ever saw me in any movie and that I ever was Bob Hope's favorite blonde, although there's nothing wrong with that, I may say. But now, will you allow me to be very simply the woman who, with millions of others, was involved in the rather disconcerting business of war that went on in Europe between the years 1939 and 1945, and who stayed on to work with the unhappy child victims of the war.

Believe it or not, I'd sooner not talk about myself, but I feel to make things clearer I should tell you a little of some of the discoveries I made during that troubled time, so that you will understand why I am here today, and why I have constituted myself a "one-woman Children's Crusade."

As some of you may know, I spent most of the war years in US hospitals in Italy and France as a Red Cross hospital worker and saw during that time the most tragic aspect of war. For years, my daily associates were men with broken bodies and broken minds, faces burned black in a plane that came down in flames, trunks without legs or arms or both. But it was not until the end of the war that I saw a sight which will be forever engraved on my memory, and which proved to be a turning point in my life. I was in Paris, on leave for a few days from my hospital train, and I was invited by some French students to go with them and help entertain soldiers in a hospital for what the French call the Gueules Cassese—the broken faces—or more factually those who for the most part have little or no faces left. Nursing is not my profession, but I had seen enough during the preceding years to know how to brace myself in such circumstances, and all went very well as I greeted one by one the tragic patients whom we had come to entertain until I came to the end of the line and met the children with no faces. And there, only the most superhuman effort on my part kept me from crying out in horror and shame that this should have been done to children. These children were the victims of civilian bombardments. They are everywhere in Europe, and in Asia, wherever war has passed. I have told you of them, because the eyes of a child burning out of a shapeless mass that once was a child's face will perhaps make you better understand the problem we are discussing today—more than would all the statistics on malnutrition and the incidence of tuberculosis, etc.

But how can I make you feel the shame I felt as an adult before the accusing eyes of these faceless children that, we in the wisdom of our superior years, had not had either the energy or the enlightenment to avoid the tragedy of war for them. How can any one of us adults feel that we do not owe these children and all like them who have suffered from war, a terrible debt? This I know was in 1945, four years ago. But how are things today? Allow me to read to you the words of a *New York Times* woman correspondent lately returned from Europe:

This is a picture of the children of Europe four years after a war that showed them no mercy and brought them no peace. For the past three months I have toured countries on both sides of the Iron Curtain, and I have seen children suffering as children were never meant to suffer. On city streets, in war orphanages, in crowded homes for mutilated children, in backward mountain villages, in caves and pillboxes 'converted' to living quarters, in tuberculosis sanitaria and congested general hospitals, this is apparent: the aftermath of Hitler's genocidal war against the youngest generation is still huge and terrifying.

Three years after the war, millions of children are still on hunger rations. Many hardly remember what a hot, nourishing meal tastes like, save as a brief luxury of UNRRA (United Nations Relief and Rehabilitation Administration) liberation days. Many have never known what milk looks like. Their thin, undersized bodies and pale, patient faces reflect the cruel logic of the occupation and war years.

For these are the youngsters who suffered first from systematic malnutrition for at least six years before peace came; then, after the war, took the same potluck as their families, living where and how they could. Thus, thousands of children, ragged and barefoot, still live in wartime bunkers, bombed-out houses and dank cellars below the bombed buildings. Hundreds of thousands are orphans who live in makeshift institutions, little old wise people following a weary routine. Uncounted thousands wait in special centers for artificial limbs which have never come to replace arms, hands, and legs.

Others are perhaps worse off—the homeless and abandoned who travel a dozen kilometers a day to wherever they hear of food and a bed. Nor is the limping army without its own social outcasts—the professional beggars and child prostitutes who, having lived by their wits during the war for self-survival, still ply their old

> trades on the streets and black markets. And over them all, threatening further their precarious existence, hangs the 'white plague,' which thrives on malnutrition and neglect—tuberculosis.
>
> This is the physical picture of the children. Psychologically, the wounds go deeper for, as Dickens has observed, 'In the little world in which children have their existence, there is nothing so finely perceived and so finely felt as injustice.'

If the General Assembly of the United Nations, which is to consider the problem next month, does not realize what is happening to the children, the children themselves do. They don't say it with words, of course. Unlike youngsters accustomed to love and care, they have forgotten, or perhaps they never knew, the age-old privilege of children to ask. But their thin and broken bodies and the rags they wear speak eloquently for them. "The obvious needs are food, milk, cod liver oil, clothes, shoes—the basic necessities—but who will supply them adequately?"

Let us reawaken and reexamine our consciences sincerely and honestly. And I don't mean automatically and wearily put our hands into our pockets, yet again for the dollar, which temporarily appeases the conscience. I am not here today to appeal for money, but more seriously to ask you—every one of you—"What are we going to do about it?"

Firstly, I'll tell you what I did, since I did what any one of you would have done when faced with the distress and the problems of so many unhappy children. I decided after the war to stay on in Europe and do the little that one individual could do to alleviate the immediate misery around me. It was a pretty hopeless business from the first, and soon it was only too obvious that I had to find another way to help.

I came back home to America and was fortunate to be asked to work with the United Nations International Children's Emergency Fund better known as UNICEF. You know their story and how they have helped to rescue so many of the world's children in the race against death. The initial effort was by UNRRA, which ended its activities in June, 1947. When it ceased operations, 11 million dollars of its assets were transferred to the UNICEF.

Because of limited resources, the present program is reduced mainly to providing special protective foodstuffs to meet the serious cases of malnutrition in the war-ravaged countries. A single supplementary ration is being distributed daily to 4,000,000 children in 12 countries of Europe and to 700,000 in China. It consists of 240 calories of fats and 60 calories of meat. This, of course, is not a sustaining diet. But it is saving millions of lives. Limited medical aid has been made available through the fund. With the cooperation of the World Health Organization, mass vaccination programs are assisting government to check the spread of tuberculosis among the child population.

But as was the case of UNRRA, so it is with UNICEF—it is only a drop of water in the bucket. It has done a fine job with what limited funds it had at its disposal, but at best it could only look after a small fraction of the world's unhappy children, and now there is reason to believe that even this help must shortly be discontinued.

The problem, fellow human beings, is plopped right back into our laps. But if you will stop to consider, just for a few minutes, some of its aspects, and the terribly important political and social implication inherent in it, I think you will realize that it is very much our problem, and that we better start right in thinking about it, as such.

I want you first of all to think of your own children. That shouldn't be too difficult! It always delighted me, in the hospital trains, to have the same experiences every time I'd meet another new GI. Immediately after the first brash introductory remarks of a rather wolfish nature, the proud parent would emerge from the "wolf's clothing" and present me with the rather battered snapshot of "junior."

You do a great deal for your children. In every way that you know, you try to ensure that their bodies shall be healthy and strong, that their education he the best you can give them, but how much do you think of the world in which they are going to live and work? How often do you Rotarians think of the Fourth Objective of Rotary?—"The advancement of international understanding, good will and peace through a world fellowship of business and professional men united in the ideal of service."

This world fellowship for your children is composed potentially of all the children growing up in all the countries of the world—children growing up happily and healthily as are your own, or else growing up as many of the German children grew up after the last war with a sense of bitterness, frustration, and injustice, which was such good ground for the growth of fascism and communism.

Our first job is surely to look after the physical and material needs of the child victims of the war, irrespective of race, color, or creed and in so doing, prove to them the reality and greatness of our democratic principles.

We must win these children to our side. They must be our children's friends. They must at least have a chance to see the way Democracy works, because I can assure you from bitter personal experience that the voice of the totalitarians is not silent. Those children, if we let them grow up with a sense of injustice, will be your children's enemies, and they will form yet another military machine to menace peace in your children's lifetime.

It is vital that we help them therefore—we the people—and that we take the leadership in a new and dynamic crusade. Where governments have failed, we being more personally involved, can win. The press, time and time again, has urged the public to take action. A recent editorial in *The New York Times* says: "Americans, with just a little imagination, can surely see the challenge." But that is hardly enough. What is needed is the impatience born of decision—articulate demand that this challenge be met with real action. It is true that the UN's International Children's Emergency Fund is giving a measure of help to some 4,500,000 children in Europe and in China, chiefly with dried skim milk and some canned meat and fish. But seven times that number in Europe alone are in immediate critical need of supplemental feeding, and the question is, must they suffer and sicken because governments have fallen down on their contributions to the Children's Fund? It is not enough to point out that the American government has given more than other governments, as indeed it has. For the contribution is still woefully small compared with the need. Nor is it enough to sit idly by and condemn leading South American countries for ignoring their obligations and contributing not a penny while supporting the Children's Fund in principle, as indeed they must be condemned. Rather, it is for Americans who do care about children to show their concern by getting actively into this fight against disease and malnutrition, which finally are a threat to their own children.

On December 11, 1946, the General Assembly of the United Nations, in creating the Children's Fund, expressed "the earnest hope that governments, voluntary agencies, and private individuals will give the Fund their generous support." Because of the failure of the national campaign to support the United Nations Appeal for Children, which was an appeal to individuals, private Americans have not had a true opportunity to express themselves. But surely it is not too late for the American people to demand that they be allowed to serve the cause with honor. If, as it seems, UNICEF is to fold up, something must take its place and immediately—unless of course, you and I can sleep happily in our beds at night when millions of children are allowed to suffer and die.

The conscience of the world is not sleeping, fortunately! In England there has been organized the World Community Chest for Children, which works through existing organizations in all countries, forming a committee with representatives of these organizations and interested individuals within each country. It works in close contact with UNICEF, UNESCO, the Red Cross and other international associations. This committee is composed of volunteers; they have a head office in London with six paid secretaries, and that is the extent of their overhead. You see, it does not need a large bureaucracy and heavy overhead to make a thing like this work. It needs enthusiasm and a burning belief in a cause, all of which I know exists here, if only we have the energy to harness it and put it to work.

I know, from my own very small experience, that since I proposed a resolution to the US Committee of the UNICEF that there be constituted an International Children's Day, there has come to me from people in many countries, the most heartening encouragement. People all over the world, like you and me, want to do something for the children and it seems to me that if we could reach out to each other and join hands, we would constitute such a force that the problem before us today would very soon cease being a problem.

I am only one woman, and will be remembered probably only because I loved children and tried to find a way to help them. I would not presume to tell as important and powerful an organization as you, what you should do. I can only make a few humble suggestions. You are powerful and you are many; you can really help the children of the world. I know that your organization has a very special interest in youth. I know, for instance that just before the outbreak of war, you were considering chartering a ship which would affect regular exchanges of young people between Europe and the States. Even then, certain among you had realized that, with our boundaries and frontiers shrinking every day, if we are to survive this era, we must learn to think of ourselves as part of a world family.

Rotarians, use all the good influence you have in your community to persuade the educational authorities, the parent-teacher associations and all such organizations to redouble their efforts in the teaching of better international understanding and good will. There is, I have discovered quite recently, a tendency in the high schools, for instance, to cut down on the teaching of foreign languages. An official of the New York Board of Regents recently announced: "We should give more job training and less importance to liberal arts in the secondary schools."

My younger sister learned how to be a very excellent typist but was killed at her typewriter by a direct hit from a German bomb in London's 1941 Blitz. It seems to me that had the generation previous to hers been more interested in encouraging good neighborliness between countries, there would have been a chance my sister might be alive today.

I am emphasizing all this because I have a very strong feeling about this new generation of children growing up today. I see in them not at all the generation of bobby-soxers, which preceded them. On the contrary, I am amazed at their seriousness and their readiness to learn more and more about the world they are to live in. It is our duty to do all in our power to see that this knowledge is made available to them so that they may still further be conditioned to the responsibilities that lie ahead.

Let us give them yet more responsibility and a greater participation, especially in any plans for a new Children's Crusade. I believe that they can succeed where we adults have so miserably failed.

As Franklin Delano Roosevelt said, when speaking to the International Student Assembly in 1942:

> Before the First World War, very few people in any country believed that youth had the right to speak for itself as a group, or to participate in councils of state. We have learned much since then. We know that wisdom does not come necessarily with years; that old men may be foolish, and young men may be wise. But in every war, it is the younger generation which bears the burden of

combat and inherits all the ills that war leaves in its wake.

It was because I believe so strongly in the youth of today that I would like to suggest and even urge the inauguration of an International Children's Day as a sort of spearhead to a new and challenging campaign: one which should have color, drama, and new meaning.

On such a day, children all over the world would unite in a common aim: to help the less fortunate ones among themselves. You, ladies and gentlemen of Rotary, can bring this small idea of mine back to your communities and nurse it into growth; you can start an international understanding of children by encouraging your own children to understand and help children of their own age in their own towns, less fortunate, of different classes, of different racial strain, or religious beliefs. And I believe the example of their sincerity and earnestness would prove salutary to those of us whose consciences have become dulled.

Someone must help the children. Are we going to leave this job to the Fascists so that they may organize yet another black, green, or brown-shirted horde; or to the Communists; or shall we, before it is too late, grasp at those extended hands all over the world, and give them the opportunity of seeing how Democracy goes to work to save the children?

Mr. Dag Hammarskjold, Second Secretary-General of the United Nations Addresses Rotary International's 50th Convention at Madison Square Garden in New York City, June 1959

Dag Hammarskjöld was Secretary-General of the United Nations from April 1953 until September 1961 when he died in a plane crash while on a UN mission in the Congo. He completed a Bachelor of Arts degree, majoring in Linguistics, Literature and History, and he continued his studies at the same university for two more years and completed a Bachelor of Laws degree in 1930. His doctoral thesis in Economics, entitled, "Konjunkturspridningen" (The Spread of the Business Cycle) earned him, in 1933, a doctorate degree from the University of Stockholm, where he assumed the responsibilities of Assistant Professor of Political Economics.

After having served one year as Secretary of the National Bank of Sweden, Mr. Hammarskjöld was appointed to the post of Permanent Under-Secretary of the Ministry of Finance. In 1949, he was appointed Secretary-General of the Foreign Office and in 1951, he became Deputy Foreign Minister.

He was appointed Acting Chairman of his country's delegation to the Seventh General Assembly in New York in 1952-1953. Mr. Hammarskjöld was unanimously nominated to be Secretary-General of the United Nations by the General Assembly in 1953 for a term of five years. He was reappointed unanimously for another five-year term in September 1957.

He held honorary degrees from Oxford University, England; in the United States from Harvard, Yale, Princeton, Columbia, the University of Pennsylvania, Amherst, John Hopkins, the University of California, Uppsala College, and Ohio University; and in Canada from Carleton College and McGill University.

I am happy to have this opportunity to address this convention of Rotary International. The aims and ideals of Rotary create a natural link to you for us who work for the United Nations. A good Rotarian, I think, is bound to be a good internationalist.

In that connection, I wish first of all to thank you for the active support which Rotarians are giving in many countries to the promotion of the World Refugee Year. This worldwide program, to give help to refugees who seek homes and a fresh start in life, begins this month. It is a program in which many governments, voluntary organizations and individuals are joining hands in response to a resolution of the United Nations General Assembly. Let us hope that this special effort will permit us to meet more adequately the human challenge of the continued presence in our midst, after many years of many millions of homeless people.

Such undertakings as the World Refugee Year reflect in one special field what I believe to be a very significant development of the years since the end of the Second World War I have in mind the widespread growth of a new sense of international responsibility, the beginnings of an international conscience. This conscience, and the efforts to which it has prompted peoples and governments, has found natural focal points in the United Nations and its related world agencies. There, it is facing no greater practical task than the economic and social development in the vast areas of Asia and Africa. I would like to share with you this morning some thoughts about this task as viewed from the vantage point of the United Nations. In view of the ideals of Rotary, I believe this is something which may be close to your hearts.

The emergence of a new international awareness has coincided with the awakening of Asia. In the postwar period, nations of Asia, which had been for many decades, in some cases even centuries under colonial rule, have achieved their political freedom. The United Nations was instrumental in many cases in helping these countries to reach this goal.

We see a similar process in motion in Africa. Many African countries are becoming independent and entering the United Nations as members. This has taken place, and is taking place, not only in respect of countries formerly under colonial rule, but also in respect of most territories for which the United Nations has a more direct responsibility.

In all these newly independent countries, it is increasingly realized that political freedom requires for its healthy growth the achievement also of other freedoms, such as freedom from want. There is a surging tide of restlessness in these countries. This is a fact we all have to reckon with. It is in the interest of the international solidarity, on which we must build the future, that the legitimate aspirations of these countries be satisfied.

We are living in an age where technological change has abolished distance. It is no longer possible for the poet to think of the silver sea as "a moat defensive to a house, against the envy of less happier lands." In the world of today, no country can isolate itself and make a little world of its own, shielded from the envy of "less happier lands." It is legitimate that every country should wish to achieve higher levels of prosperity. But for rich and poor countries alike, prosperity cannot be assured in the long run unless there is a forward movement on a broad front, so that all share in the progress and no country builds its wealth on the sacrifices of others.

It is a painful fact that in the economic field, the gap, already wide between the prosperous countries and those less fortunate, is steadily becoming wider. Economists have commented on this phenomenon, analyzed the reasons for it and have suggested remedies. While all those remedies call for a maximal effort on the part of the less advanced countries, they also call for a new sense of responsibility and a heightened desire to help on the part of those more fortunate. If such reactions do not find expression in practical and constructive action, there is bound to be a danger of instability in the poorer countries, which would reflect on the political world situation.

It is the responsibility of the international community to pursue a policy of solidarity so that such situations do not develop. It is our duty to assist the countries, which now are at a serious disadvantage in making an inventory of their own resources, and in diagnosing the reasons for their economic difficulties, to suggest appropriate remedies. Furthermore, it is also our responsibility to see that, where outside help is essential in stimulating the process and accelerating the pace of economic development, this help is given readily in the form and manner and at the time when it could do the most good.

The demographers tell us that it took the world thousands of years for its population to reach the billion mark, but only 100 years to add the second billion. It is now estimated that based on present trends, it will take only 30 years to add a third billion. Yet, another billion or two may be added before mankind achieves a balance in the population field.

The biggest contributor to this rapid population growth has been Asia. This complicates the problem of economic development there in various ways. Among other things, it makes it necessary for the countries of Asia to achieve a much higher rate of increase of national product annually than would otherwise be necessary, in order to ensure that the impact of the economic development on living standards is not altogether lost. To maintain the necessary momentum of economic development, it is not possible for these countries to go forward exclusively on their own steam.

Some of these ancient lands of Asia were the most advanced countries of the world not too many centuries ago. If the scales have now been turned in favor of the West, a main cause has been the industrial revolution which has taken place there with the subsequent development of technology. This change coincided in point of time with the growth of colonialism. The historic pattern of trade between Asia and Europe on a basis of equality gave place to a different relationship. The Asian countries came mainly to serve as sources of raw materials and consumers of finished goods. The time now seems to be ripe for some transfer, to the benefit of all, of resources, both human and material, in the opposite direction.

Such a transfer is not as simple as it might sound. This is especially true when technology has to be transplanted in practically every case; problems of adaptation are bound to arise, which have to take into account various factors at the other end. To give an example, advanced technology involving intensive use of capital and of laborsaving machinery is obviously not well suited to the needs of countries facing acute problems of surplus labor and unemployment. The problem of adaptation arises not only in regard to the transfer of technology, but in finding solutions for practically every problem of economic and social development. For example, answers to the population problem in these countries have to take into account important social and religious factors as well as political factors different from those experienced in the West.

As a matter of course, serious consideration should be given to the specific traditions of these countries. It is important that they should be respected. Plain living and high thinking (the two do not necessarily go together) are often the ideals. This may sometimes make for a somewhat too ready acceptance of austerity, which, however, is no excuse for acquiescence by governments and leaders in an inhuman state of poverty. Whatever the ideals, there is everywhere to be found an urge to improve living standards—an urge which we all share.

The things that should be taken up first are obviously not only purely physical things like food, clothing, and shelter, but also a healthy environment and facilities for education. If there is a steady and visible improvement, year by year, in these basic facilities, then the people can hold their heads high, secure in the knowledge that progress to a dignified life is being made and maintained. This is something rather different from the creation of artificial needs, and the technological innovation to meet those needs, which is characteristic of more affluent societies.

It is essential that no economically underdeveloped country should overlook, or even temporarily forget, the sense of discipline and the effort and sacrifice, which are required in order to achieve a better way of life. But, provided these conditions exist, the international community should be conscious of the need for its help, and of its obligation to make available the resources and know-how, which the poorer countries must have if we are to achieve such progress along the broad front as is necessary and in the best interest of all.

The Asian countries will need a great thrust in the acceleration of their economic development, especially in these early stages, just as an aircraft does before the take-off stage is reached; as you know, thereafter the cruising may require less power. However, the road to economic development is perhaps more like the long and hard trek up a mountain than an airport runway. Let us be encouraged by the fact that, in this case, each mile on the long road up the mountain should make the next mile just a little easier. And all along the way, if we have eyes to see, there will be vistas of improving living conditions for millions of people.

The problems of Africa have their own special aspects. Vast resources exist in that great continent, without great pressure of population. Even vaster resources will no doubt be uncovered in the course of time. Here the primary need may be for technological training and social evolution, as also for development of methods for better mobilization and exploitation of their available material resources. Except for this important difference, most of my observations probably apply to Africa with equal force.

As I have pointed out, the policy required from more advanced countries would reflect on international solidarity, which in turn finds a strong justification in their own enlightened self-interest. Whether it is bilateral aid, or contributions to international funds, the taxpayer's pocketbook is touched, and he is entitled to ask what value he is receiving for his money. To this question there is no simple answer; but I would like to think that the sense of international responsibility, which prompts such assistance to the less advanced countries is only the elevation to the international plane of the basic principles of social justice, which are now accepted as axiomatic at the national level, irrespective of systems of thinking.

It is now generally understood that no country can afford to have areas of poverty and depression within its own frontiers, and that social justice demands that the national resources be deployed for the uplift of such areas. The process, of course, is a continuous one within national boundaries. The same holds good, I think, of the international community. All the values that we cherish will be jeopardized if we do not face up to this simple fact. This conception is basic to the work of the United Nations in the economic and social field.

I referred just now to enlightened self-interest. Let me elaborate. It is obvious that the economically less developed countries are potentially the greatest markets for the products of the advanced countries. With rising standards of living in the less developed countries, we may be able to establish a circle—an ever growing one in fact—of greater exchange of goods amongst the nations of the world and higher standards of living for all.

In this process, patterns of trade may change and countries, which are now importing simple consumer goods may be needing the most complex of advanced machines. It is comparatively easy for the advanced countries to reorganize their production in this way to meet changing needs. I would, therefore, hold that the policy, which seems indicated by the situation facing us in Asia and Africa, is one which provides good value in the long run for those whose pocketbooks are touched.

In this gathering of Rotary International are Rotarians from every part of the world, including the countries of Asia and Africa of whose problems I have just spoken, as well as the representatives of countries whose pocketbooks are touched. It is worth remembering that even the poorest of us have something to give, and the richest among us have something to receive. This is amply proved also by the exchange of experience for which the United Nations has provided and can provide ever growing opportunities.

I have spoken of some economic aspects of the emerging international solidarity, which is served by the United Nations. In the work of the International Bank of the United Nations Technical Assistance Program, of the regional United Nations Commissions for Latin America, Europe, Asia, the Far East and Africa, of the United Nations Special Fund for economic development in many other ways there is a new and fundamentally significant development in world affairs. So far, the allocation of resources by the nations to this work has regretfully been far below both their capacity and the need. But it is more important to recognize the significance of the fact that the sense of international solidarity, and that means, of course, human solidarity—in this way—is beginning to make itself felt as an important factor in world affairs.

The hopes for peace rest upon a further development of this sense of international solidarity and upon an understanding of how it may best be translated into practical terms applicable to the world in which we live.

I have spoken here about economic matters mainly. This should not make us forget the special values of the United Nations as an instrument of negotiation, be it between the Atlantic Alliance and the Communist Alliance, or between the traditional West and the new countries of Asia and Africa, or perhaps among countries within any one of these groups or regions. But political, economic and social factors are inseparable parts of the whole development. When we try to translate the emerging sense of international solidarity from thoughts into words, and from words into deeds, we should remember that a policy of reconciliation requires of us that we face our tasks in the economic and social fields, just as economic progress requires unrelenting efforts to solve the political problems. The international conscience is reflected in our actions over the whole range of international problems, and if we do not start with the simple questions of how to provide everybody with his daily bread, the rest of our efforts are likely to be of little avail.

Your mission in Rotary "seek and to apply all that which brings people together" in the wider and deeper sense about which the new international conscience tells us, is also the goal of the United Nations.

The Following Conversations with the Ambassadors were held between 2004 and 2016

The German Mission, German Ambassador, Dr. Wolfgang Trautwein

The German Mission had graciously provided the ideal venue for the Rotary Club of New York's monthly International Breakfast Meeting at the German House from 2003 to 2010, for which we were all very grateful. Dr. Trautwein generously donated the revenue from the breakfast meeting to the Rotary Club of New York's Foundation. The Ambassador candidly admitted that before being reassigned to New York, he knew about Rotary but did not realize how engaged and committed Rotarians were. As such, he expressed how grateful he was to be invited as a full member in the Rotary Club of New York and that he expected to continue being a Rotarian even when assigned to another part of the world.

Fellow Rotarian and Deputy Permanent Representative of Germany to the United Nations, Dr. Wolfgang Trautwein, attended school in Düsseldorf and studied law at the University of Saarbrücken and University College in London earning a PhD in law. In 1976, he joined the German Foreign Service. In 1983, he served in Tel Aviv. In 1992-97, he was head of the Legal and Consular Affairs Division as Consul General in London. In 2001-2003, he headed the North Africa and Near–East Affairs Department in Berlin. Since August 2003, he has served in New York as Deputy Representative to the UN for Germany.

Dr. Trautwein informed us that while many New Yorkers were spending their summer vacations and long weekends at the beach or in the mountains, the UN community was very busy preparing for the September Summit and producing the Outcome Document.

Permanent Mission of the Federal Republic of Germany to the United Nations, Michael von Ungern-Sternberg, Minister Plenipotentiary

Iraq Road Map—One Year Later

The following remarks were part of a discussion that took place at the monthly International Breakfast Meeting of the International Service Division of the Rotary Club of New York. The meeting was held on April 21, 2004 at the German Permanent Mission to the United Nations in New York City. This is a condensed and edited text made available as a resource to update Rotarians on current issues facing the International Development Community. The meeting was opened and moderated by Mr. Sylvan M. Barnet.

MR. BARNET: Why are Rotarians interested in this topic this morning?

We are a peace organization, and peace and conflict resolution is one of the areas we work in. But we are also a social and humanitarian organization. And the work that we do cannot be done in areas of conflict. We are waiting for the Security Council, the Secretary-General, and a lot of others to make it safe for us to go back to Iraq and do our social and humanitarian work.

I should mention that we got a fabulous report from Afghanistan where Rotary is deeply involved in education and health projects. So, we hope that we will be back in Baghdad soon so we can continue our work there too. It is very appropriate that we are meeting here to get an update on the "Road Map" for Iraq. It is one year and one month after we were briefed by the German Deputy Ambassador, Hans Schumacher, on what was going to happen or did not happen at the Security Council on March 19, 2003.

Now, I will briefly tell you about our guest speaker. Mr. Michael von Ungern-Sternberg is the Minister Plenipotentiary of the Permanent Mission of the Federal Republic of Germany to the United Nations. He has been with the German Foreign Office for twenty-two years with posts in Bonn, Morocco, the Soviet Union, and EU (European Union) in Brussels. In 1998, he headed the Division of EU Enlargement in the Foreign Office, and for the last two years he has headed the Political Section of this Permanent Mission of Germany.

MR. UNGERN-STERNBERG: Thank you very much Mr. Barnet. It is a pleasure to be here. It has been one year since Ambassador Schumacher was here and as you know a lot of things have been going on. But to start with, I would like to say that I was struck by the invitation I got from you. You identified the problem in a very intelligent way. You said, "We are looking forward to going into Iraq and opening up Rotary Clubs." No one, I thought, has ever looked at the problem that way. But it might be quite a good measure to use because as soon as Rotary can be in Iraq, then civil society will be functioning, and civility will be back. So maybe it is really a good way of looking at the problem. We are all looking forward for Rotary coming into Iraq!

Immediately after the war, everyone said let's get over our differences in the Security Council and rebuild Iraq. Nevertheless, lots of differences have still persisted. In fact, what we have seen in the last few days is that Spain has pulled its troops out of Iraq, and other countries are thinking of also pulling out because the area has become very risky.

The United States, as well as the United Kingdom, have put enormous political and financial efforts into Iraq, yet the coalition has not seen the result they were expecting or hoping to see. If you compare this to Afghanistan, where the situation was also very bad, everyone acknowledges that a lot of progress has been achieved and the situation has been stabilized. Just two weeks ago, we had a conference in Berlin on Afghanistan. The United States was very happy with the results and more importantly, Afghanis were also very happy. There seems to be light at the end of the tunnel!

What has happened in Afghanistan to make it work, more or less, that did not happen in Iraq? To sum up right from the beginning, the big issue is legitimacy and ownership of the populations and of the political elite. That is what was handled differently from the Afghanistan case. In the last year, we have seen the coalition going in and running Iraq and taking control.

"Road-Map" was the exact term used by the Germans and the French at the Security Council last year. It suggested that the UN work on the Road Map together with the Iraqis, present a possible road-map for the political process to the Security Council, and take it from there. But this proposal was rejected by the coalition because it wanted to stay in control. It did not want international participation.

In September, Paul Bremer, the US Administrator in Iraq, presented his seven-point plan. There was no exit time frame, but a transfer of sovereignty was only foreseen at the very end of the plan. The immediate response by the Secretary-General, the Special Envoy of the UN to Iraq, Mr. Brahimi, and others, was that this would make things difficult because in Iraq and the Arab world, people would not perceive this as trying to increase ownership.

On the 15th of November, the seven-point plan was revised and there was a new agreement between the governing council, which is composed of twenty-five Iraqis, and the CPA (Coalition Provisional Authority). They set out a different plan that outlined the main events to take place to hand over sovereignty and spelled out the TAL (Transitional Administrative Law). Among others, an agreement regarding the status of the troops of the multinational coalition on one side, and the governing council on the other side, was to be reached by the CPA. This raised some suspicion because some people were saying, "why have an agreement with the governing council instead of having it with the interim government that will be formed under this agreement over the summer?"

In addition, when the TAL was adopted under this agreement, some of the members of the governing council refused to sign it because several of the main stakeholders in Iraq, the Shiites and Ayatollah Sistani, could not accept some of the provisions. Eventually, however, after a lot of background negotiations, this Transitional Administrative Law was adopted.

If one looks at the contents of the TAL, it is a really impressive piece of legislative work. It contains human and fundamental rights, and in our estimation, many other positive elements. It states that when the permanent constitution is accepted, there would be a right of veto if three governorates would not give their consent.

The Shiites were concerned that if the permanent constitution would not give the Kurds what they wanted, they could easily reject it because they had a strong majority. And the Shiites have said that they were going to be dependent on Kurdish vetoes. This is a fundamental problem with the TAL because the Kurds now had a document that they considered binding, and on the other side, the Shiites were confronted with something they didn't like, but their representatives in the governing council had signed on to. So, there was a serious problem when you look at the constitutional process.

So, what is the way ahead, and what are the risks now?

First, we are faced with a growing anti-foreign tendency, and growing anti-Americanism, in particular. There is increased apprehension by any foreigner wanting to go into Iraq. As we can see, all nationalities are getting kidnapped and killed, and it is becoming a more dangerous place for international involvement. This is going to hamper the political process.

Second, we are going to face serious problems among the ethnic groups in Iraq. In the aftermath of Hussein, every group was somewhat relieved, except some smaller minorities. There was a sincere will to move on and try to find a new way to reconstruct Iraq into a unified country. But, now the divisions have grown more important, and divergent interests have appeared in a much stronger way.

Third, the neighboring countries are growing more worried because the events are not going in the right direction. This is particularly true with countries that have Kurdish minorities. We see that the Iranians are trying to get more involved, the Turks have serious apprehensions, and so do the Syrians.

Fourth, there is a major problem concerning security. Security issues and the political process are strongly linked to each other. Without security, they will never be able to achieve a certain degree of progress in the political process. At the same time, without seeing progress in the political process, there won't be any security. There is a very strong interdependence. Everyone agrees that the American forces have done, in many ways, an impressive job, but there is no way to establish security if the Iraqis do not see any progress in the political process.

Mr. Brahimi has suggested a proposal for the future that is hopeful. While he has not yet submitted it to the Security Council, his main ideas have already been in the newspapers:

First, on the 30th of June, we will have a transfer of power. And I think everyone agrees on it. The United States is interested, the Europeans are interested, and the Iraqis are interested. So, there is going to be something that will happen on the 30th of June. And this needs to be perceived by the Iraqis as something legitimate.

Second, the new government will be run by a prime minister, with a president, and two vice presidents, and there is probably going to be an ethnic and religious element. We are going to see Shiites, Sunnis, and Kurds as important figures.

Third, there is going to be a transitional assembly to hold a national convention similar to what happened in Afghanistan.

Fourth, after the national conference, there is to be an international conference with many of the major international players, such as the Coalition, neighboring states, and members of the EU.

Sometime in January, 2005, the Iraqis will have an election. Sistani has insisted on this, and Mr. Brahimi has said this is possible. This will be a major point because at that stage we have an Iraqi organization developed out of this process with a certain degree of legitimacy. Not all the problems will be over then, but at least we will have some kind of an institutional setup, which will not be contested as being an imposition by the outside world.

On the security side, many have suggested the involvement of NATO (North Atlantic Treaty Organization). This is a debate that is going on in NATO, but there are different opinions being voiced there. We are not sure if using NATO would be helpful for the following reasons:

By replacing, for example, 20,000 American troops with 20,000 French, German, Dutch, or any other European troops, the face of the security force will not be changed. It will not be perceived in Iraq as something they own, be will still be perceived as a military occupation. We are not sure if it is going to increase security. We are not sure if it will increase the image of NATO—the risk—being perceived as something that is Christian and coming from the West, as opposed to something Arabic and Islamic.

The CPA is doing all it can in developing and gearing up an Iraqi police force. However, we all agree it was a mistake to disband the Iraqi Army in the beginning. There were approximately 200,000 Iraqi soldiers, I believe, put on the street with nothing to do, and they were available to be recruited by Iraqi militia. For the sake of security, it is important to draw in some participation from the Arab world.

What can the Security Council do, and where do we stand? The British and Americans have said we need a new resolution and we all agree on this. However, we are not yet working on any text in the Security Council. The Coalition has outlined some of the main points they would like included:—the resolution should state that on the 30th of June, 2004, sovereignty will transfer to the Iraqis and it is the end of occupation. Laws that are in existence today should remain in existence as long as Iraqi authorities have not changed them.

Determine the commanders and participants of the multinational force.

This force must have the face of someone trying to stabilize the country rather than someone who is there to occupy the county. While it is not the intention of the Coalition to occupy the country, we have to accept as a political reality that it is being perceived as an occupier.

Define the role of the United Nations.

It is important for the UN to be perceived as independent of the Coalition Forces. The UN should be the main broker in the political process. This is an area that the UN has a great comparative advantage over. The UN is not perceived as pursuing any self-interest, and it has the necessary experience. A special representative of the Secretary-General, who has knowledge of the issues and is respected in the region, would be effective.

However, the Security Council resolution can only work if it gets the backing of the main players in Iraq. There is no use producing a text here in New York, if Sistani and other main players are going to reject it. Therefore, it is very important to see the 30th of June as a start of a new stage in the whole process, and that the transitional government will not be perceived as a continuation of the governing council. It is also important that other forces in the region get more involved and we gradually get a more Arab and Islamic face.

Spanish and Turkish "Alliance of Civilization" Initiative Seeking Civil Society Support

Ambassador Palacio earned his law degree from the University of Madrid, and is a graduate of the Madrid School of Diplomacy. He started his diplomatic career in 1983 and has served in Bolivia, Morocco, Brazil, and Geneva. In 2004 he was appointed Ambassador and Deputy Permanent Representative to the United Nations in New York. The Ambassador was very involved with Rotary and attended many meetings while serving in Brazil. As such, he commends Rotary as a great humanitarian organization working to improve the world.

Events of recent years have exacerbated mutual suspicion, fear, and misunderstanding between Islamic and Western societies, and this environment has been exploited by extremists throughout the world. With this in mind, when the Prime Minister of Spain, José Luis Rodríguez Zapatero was first elected in 2005, he introduced the "Alliance of Civilization" initiative to bridge the divide between Western and Islamic societies. Spain also invited a very special ally, the Prime Minister of Turkey, Recep Tayyip Erdoğan, to join the Alliance, because Turkey is a nation at the crossroads of two different worlds—the dividing line between the Eastern and Western worlds.

Ambassador Palacio pointed out that the Alliance needed to receive global legitimacy which is only attainable at the UN. Therefore, it had been presented at the 59th General Assembly and had forty members-states in support. At the same time, this being a plan for tangible actions, it asked for support from civil society, foundations, and all organizations currently working in these fields to reach out to areas of conflict and disaffection.

"Singapore's Permanent Representative to the United Nations, Ambassador Vanu Gopala Menon" *By Sheila Washington, (Visiting Rotarian from San Diego, California)*

It was Wednesday April 19th, and at 8:30 a.m. the Rotary Club NY was in session on the top floor of the German Mission. It was a beautiful spring morning for a room full of members, guests, and the keynote speaker, Ambassador Vanu Gopala Menon. The Ambassador is Singapore's Permanent Representative to the United Nations in New York, and concurrently Singapore's High Commissioner to Canada.

After an excellent breakfast, opening remarks, and announcements, Coordinator and Moderator Joe Klee of the International Division of the NYC Rotary introduced Ambassador Menon. Born in Singapore, September 8, 1960, Ambassador Menon joined the Ministry of Foreign Affairs in June 1985. He served in many leadership positions, including Singapore's Chief Negotiator for the Singapore-Australia Free Trade Agreement and Chairman of the World Trade Organization's Council for TRIPS (Trade-related Intellectual Property Rights) from 2003-2004. He presented his credentials to the United Nations in September, 2004.

In his overview, the Ambassador's comments reminded us that the UN has evolved from an institution founded to prevent war into an umbrella organization whose work today revolves around a seemly ambitious and open-ended agenda. Its scope of work includes but is not limited to: human rights, economic development, world health, child welfare, women's rights, international justice, trade, and intellectual property among other tasks. The UN has been praised for helping eliminate apartheid in South Africa, coordinating the mammoth relief effort for the 2004 tsunami in Southeast Asia, and setting benchmarks for combating global poverty, hunger and disease as part of its Millennium Development goals. It is not usual for the UN to be the first responder coordinating efforts in times of global crisis.

However, its long list of accomplishments is usually trumped by a short list of hot-button items that create and rule its image. This includes, the stronger image of the OIP (Oil-for-Food Programme) in Iraq amidst allegations of corruption, peacekeepers accused of various crimes, and its seemly ineffective Human Rights Commission.

The UN began with about 50 states. In its 60th year, there were 191 Member States. Supporters and critics alike agree that the United Nations needs an overhaul both physically and institutionally. In addition, its governance and management are under attack from many directions. The Ambassador highlighted issues for the reform process.

Building a peacekeeping force that stands on its own

In most countries, the UN has the Good Housekeeping Seal of Approval and has proved itself effective in peacekeeping efforts. Historically, small and medium-sized countries are more likely to act at the request of the UN than from an individual country. However, there is no standing UN Peacekeeping Force for timely assignment.

Restructuring of the discredited Human Rights Commission.

It currently takes a 2/3 vote to remove a state from the Commission. A change to simple majority is one of the proposals under consideration.

Investing In Development: Both developed and developing countries have a stake in development. As globalization races on, it presents new and fast-moving challenges to the Member States. In a final report to the UN in 2005, an action plan was outlined to achieve the goal to cut world poverty by half in a decade. Will the Member States seize the opportunity to take action?

Adapting True Management Reform

Secretary-General Annan announced in March a bottom-up look at how the Secretariat should be managed. The plan includes taking certain functions out of New York and implementing rigorous monitoring for more transparency of processes and procedures.

Image Building

Recalling that the United States took the lead in the creation of the UN, there is currently a substantial and vocal hostility to the UN in the United States. How can the UN promote itself in the United States?

Looking Ahead

The General Assembly remains a place for discussion and achieving consensus on these and other issues. The awesome veto power of the Security Council membership of five seems to be lessened since the end of the Cold War because there is general recognition that the world is interconnected, and for all practical purposes, has no borders. The biggest challenge ahead for these two main bodies is the selection of the next Secretary-General by the end of 2006. The outcome of that process will be most telling for the UN's future.

Creating a more effective format for explaining the UN with a common understanding of its goals for the general public's consumption is under consideration. For instance, directing some criticism directly at the Member State may be more appropriate. If a problem were to go to the Security Council and one of its members blocked meaningful action, is it fair to consider that action a failure of the UN, or for the record, is it the result of a UN State that prevented the UN from doing its job?

In summary, the Ambassador gave Rotarians a sensitive and comprehensive picture of the UN today. He expressed deeply the commitment of his country to a vital UN that can meet its challenges effectively. It was also gratifying to learn of the dedicated work of his delegation over the years to affect meaningful change that is consistent with global challenges.

On the surface, it seems that since its 60th anniversary summit, the UN is taking steps to make the adjustment needed for a comprehensive overhaul of its operating structure and management.

And so it was on a beautiful spring morning in April, as we headed off in different directions, that there was a better understanding, and just maybe the knowledge that momentum for reform can be sustained. At the UN today, the glass is half full.

The hope for a better way of life for most people on this planet is still alive.

Slovenian Ambassador, Eva Tomic, Outlines Gender Equality at the United Nations

Ambassador Eva Tomic, the Deputy Representative to the United Nations of Slovenia was the guest speaker at the International Breakfast Meeting in December, 2007. She joined the Foreign Service of Slovenia and was first assigned to New York in 1991. During her career, she headed the Department of Human Rights in Slovenia, and also worked with the International Criminal Court. In recent years, she served as the Vice Chair of the Commission on Sustainable Development, and has worked with the Third Committee of the UN which deals with social, humanitarian and cultural issues such as immigration, youth and family.

Since its independence in 1991 from the former Yugoslavia, Slovenia is one of the nine new European countries that joined the EU. And with only two million people, Ambassador Tomic is ostensibly very proud that her country has been selected to head the European Union in 2008 after Germany's leadership in 2007.

Ambassador Tomic opened the discussion by stating that the UN is well represented by gender equality agencies, but that the organization as a whole has not utilized these entities as effectively as it could. She spoke about the need for continued commitment for "gender mainstreaming" at the highest levels of the UN. In addition, the Ambassador stressed the importance of interaction between different UN branches on gender equality ("Gender Mainstreaming" is one of the strategies for achieving gender equality). It involves ensuring that gender perspectives, and attention to the goal of gender equality, are central to all activities.

Security Council Resolution 1325 (2000) also promoted the participation of women and bringing gender perspectives to the center of all United Nations peacemaking, peacekeeping, peace-building and reconstruction efforts.

The UN agencies that promote gender equality within the UN Organizational structure include:

- OSAGI—Office of Special Advisor on Gender Issues and the Advancement of Women
- UNIFEM—UN Development Fund for Women: advocates the strengthening of gender equality programming of UN operational agencies. It also conducts very effective work on the ground working with NGOs.
- INSTRAW—International Research and Training Institute for the Advancement of Women: promoted research on equity for women issues.
- CSW—Commission on the Status of Women: part of the United Nations ECOSOC (Economic and Social Council)
- UNDAW—UN Division for the Advancement of Women
- IANWGE—Inter-Agency Network on Women and Gender Equality: a network of gender focal points in UN entities. The Network is chaired by the Special Advisor on Gender Issues and

Advancement of Women.

The latest proposal of the UN Reform panel recommends the implementation of a "One UN Policy" at the country level. For example, there are twenty-four UN agencies operating in Columbia. Consequently, establishing communication or coordination of goals and objectives while incorporating gender issues into the decision process may be compromised. By merging all agencies into one, gender equality issues can be more effectively incorporated in the decision and policy-making process.

It was also pointed out by the meeting's moderator, Dr. Josef Klee, that the former Secretary-General was committed to achieving gender employment parity with 50% of the core, non-civil service posts held by women. Currently there are 2,700 "Core Posts" that have been identified to be under this quota system. At present, 43% of these posts are now held by women. While this percentage may be impressive when compared with other large organizations, it is still not parity. As a result, women now receive some advantage when applying for one of these positions. Unfortunately as expected, this creates the conundrum of not discriminating against men.

Rotary International's UN representative, Sylvan Barnet, noted that at least six of the MDGs (UN Millennium Development Goals), if not all, are particularly favorable to women. There is a "Feminization of poverty, water, and HIV/AIDS, since women are more affected by these developmental issues than men." He also noted that Rotary is very committed to incorporating women in international development as evidenced more than 50% of the one thousand Rotary Ambassadorial Scholars being women, as well as 60% of the Rotary Peace Fellows.

"Ambassador Gomez, Mexico/United States Relations" *By Shelia Washington (Visiting Rotarian from San Diego, California)*

If it's Tuesday, it must be Rotary Club of New York

It was Tuesday, Mexico Day, 2007 at the Rotary Club of New York. The Mariachis with Rotarian Rosario "Charo" De Pretti singing provided the musical atmosphere for a festive luncheon. After the Mexican and US National Anthems and the Invocation followed, President Bill Currie welcomed all to the first Mexico Day. An excellent Ensalada Tehnana (salad) whetted our appetites for the sumptuous Mexican lunch catered by Café Frida.

It was also the day to award two students with scholarships. The award citations for Ms. Alendi Vidal and Ms. Elizabeth Rozon were acknowledged as accomplished students with well-rounded civic and academic lives. They were accompanied to the stage by Deputy Consul General of Mexico Francisco Javier Diaz de Leon.

A raffle for round-trip tickets to Mexico City and dinner for two at Café Frida added to the festivities. The proceeds went to Rotary Foundation.

At first glance it was easy to expect a standard Chamber of Commerce speech from the Keynote Speaker, Ambassador Eduardo Ramos Gomez. He is President of the US Mexico Chamber of Commerce, Northwest Region, and formerly Ambassador to Singapore. However, Ambassador Gomez gave one of the most thoughtful speeches on Mexico/US relations and the North American family of nations. It was good to be reminded that Mexico is the second largest trading partner of the United States.

He highlighted four issues: Water, Health/Aids, Energy, and Emigration while emphasizing the need for a focus on health issues. He pointed out that since 9/11, Mexico/NAFTA (The North American Free Trade Agreement) have been left dangling leaving Latin America in general with a leadership vacuum. In addition, the child, NAFTA who is more than ten years old is unattended in its adolescence. The plea was, "What's the next phase to fulfill the promise for the North American family of the United States, Mexico, and Canada as conceived by the creation of NAFTA? In a quiet but compelling voice, Ambassador Gomez expressed puzzlement as to why the nations were not sitting down to talks about our common goals and common problems. However, he left us with a sense of confidence that the underlying strengths of the North American relationship, with its experience and wisdom, will win out.

Mexico Day was festive and most enjoyable even as it provided much food for thought.

Permanent Representative to Kenya, Ambassador Bahemuka

Permanent Representative to Kenya, Ambassador Bahemuka opened the conversation by thanking all Rotarians. She acknowledged her image of Rotarians as people who are proactive and quick to respond to emergencies. She praised all Rotarians around the world and especially those in her own country. In this light, she was delighted to accept the Club's invitation to formally address Rotarians.

Ambassador Bahemuka is a trained sociologist and earned her undergraduate degree at Marygrove College in Detroit, USA, and a Doctorate in Sociology from Nairobi University, Kenya. She is currently Chairperson of the Social and Human Sciences National Committee at the UNESCO (United Nations Educational, Scientific and Cultural Organization) National Commission.

She noted that there have been many reports and studies conducted determining what is needed to help Africa, but reports are only useful if they are put into action. Nevertheless, there are several essential areas that need to be improved:

- Good governance and using peer review of African governments by other African governments
- Transportation and communication infrastructure improvements
- Gender concerns, such as girls attending schools and how men and women interact with one another
- Sustainable food production
- Curtailing "Brain Drain"
- Increasing the availability of clean drinking water (Rotary is very helpful and active.)
- Debt cancellation is needed because many countries are unable to pay back their loans, and much of the assistance was given to a few companies and individuals.

Africa is capable of producing a number of raw materials and food products but non-African governmental trade barriers make it difficult to sell these products.

But most importantly she urged Rotarians not to wait for the great projects. She advised them to: "Put up one light. Don't wait for the big project to brighten all of Africa. Provide the small but consistently implemented projects, one by one, and brighten an African corner."

The Consul General of India in New York, the Honorable Neelam Deo

The Consul General of India in New York, the Honorable Neelam Deo provided an impressive summary and analysis of her country's economic growth and cultural contributions over the last decade. She gave her presentation at the Rotary Club of New York's lunch meeting held at the Harvard Club.

Ms. Neelam Deo was appointed the Consul General of India, New York in October, 2005. She has a Master's Degree in Economics from the Delhi School of Economics and had taught in Kamala Nehru College, Delhi University. As a career diplomat of the Indian Foreign Service with over three decades in the Indian Diplomatic Corps, Ms. Deo has been India's Ambassador to Denmark and the Ivory Coast, with concurrent accreditation to Sierra Leone, Niger, and Guinea. Prior to her assignment in New York, she was Head of the Bangladesh, Sri Lanka, and Myanmar Division in the Ministry of External Affairs, New Delhi, where she dealt with India's overall relations with these countries. Ms. Deo has also worked in India's Diplomatic Missions in Washington, D.C., Bangkok, and Rome.

The relationship between the world's largest democracy and the USA is strong and includes the following examples:

- The largest number of international university students in the United States is from India.
- Ten percent of the CEOs of the top 250 US companies are Indian.
- Fifty percent of start-up entrepreneurs in Silicon Valley are from India.
- The $2,500 car in India will change the way cars are manufactured.
- Indian film and media writers, many who have studied in American universities, are very successful in the United States.
- Some of the earliest Indian classic works of literature such as the Hindu epics Ramayana and Mahabharata, treatises such as Vaastu Shastra in architecture and town planning, and Arthashastra in political science are becoming increasingly known in Western countries.
- It was also mentioned that there are more than 2,100 Rotary

Clubs in India, the third largest number of clubs after the United States and Japan.

United States Ambassador, John Bolton, Outlines Key United Nations' Concerns

December 5, 2006 was the day when most of the nation's editorial pages were either praising *(Wall Street Journal)* or condemning *(The New York Times)* United States Ambassador to the United Nations, John Bolton, on his one year tenure at the United Nations. Nevertheless, he was enthusiastically welcomed at the Rotary Club of New York when he graciously spent his lunch hour discussing the key priorities that the United States faces at the United Nations.

The Ambassador emphasized that there is a full agenda at the UN, particularly at the Security Council. The most pressing problems are the deliverable nuclear weapons programs being developed by North Korea and Iran. In 1994, North Korea signed an agreement to stop its nuclear weapon development program in exchange for generous economic benefits. However, it is now being purported that North Korea has been clandestinely engaged in, and benefiting from, Iran's nuclear program.

According to the Ambassador, North Korea sells ballistic missile technology and weapons to outlaw states. It also is earning foreign currency by counterfeiting US currency, laundering illegal gambling revenue from Japan, and selling illegal drugs through diplomatic pouches. As a consequence, the UN Security Council passed Resolution 1695, which demands suspension of all related ballistic missile activity and urges North Korea to return immediately to Six-Party Talks without precondition. The Council also passed Resolution 1718, which prevents provision of nuclear technology, large-scale weapons, and luxury goods to the country, and permits inspection of cargo to ensure compliance. This is also designed to impede Kim Jong-Il's ability to reward his subordinates, the Ambassador noted.

Perhaps more problematic is Iran. With its uranium mines, and uranium enrichment production facilities, Iran has mastered, or is very close to mastering, the nuclear fuel cycle and may already have an indigenous capability to develop nuclear weapons. For four years, the United States has been trying to convince European, Russian, and

Chinese leaders to stop Iran's nuclear weapon capabilities before they have full nuclear weapon capability. Security Council members have been willing to invite Iran to join the rest of the federalized world if they give up their pursuit of a weapons-grade nuclear program. However, since there was no progress in these discussions, the Security Council passed a resolution for Iran to cease its uranium enrichment program by last August 31, 2008.

Many Member States at the UN are frustrated by continuing the diplomatic route for too long, and sanctions are now being considered. It will be a test of the Security Council to see if it will take this issue seriously. If it does not, the United States will need to consider alternate means to stop nuclear weapon capability in Iran, Ambassador Bolton affirmed.

Another area of concern is the influence of Hezbollah relative to the democratically elected government of Lebanon. The Ambassador stated that Syria is encouraging the Lebanese governments to concede power to Hezbollah. Close to 25% of Lebanon's population has demonstrated in the streets in support of Hezbollah, but political parties should not have their own militia, the Ambassador emphasized. If the democratically elected government does not survive, Hezbollah will acquire control of Lebanon's governmental assets and its military. Consequently, Syria and Iran will be very influential with Hezbollah, and then there will be a "terrorist" state in the Middle East.

Another point is that the government of Sudan is still resisting UN Peacekeeping Force to stop gross violations of human rights, starvation, and murder in Darfur, he noted. During the Q&A section of his address, Ambassador Bolton did acknowledge that the United Nations is and has been successful in a number of areas, but he advised, as Paul Volker did in last year's UN Reform Report, that the UN has to be sure it does not get lost in a "Culture of Inaction."

Representative to the United Nations for South Korea, H.E. Mr. Kim Bong-hyun

Representative to the United Nations for South Korea, H.E. Mr. KIM Bong-hyun, the Deputy Permanent, was the guest speaker at the July 2009 International Breakfast Meeting of the Rotary Club of New York. After studying in Korea, Ambassador Kim received a master's degree from the University of Illinois in 1982, and has served in posts in Japan, the Russian Federation, and Pakistan. He also shared with the Rotarians that he had just completed his PhD. During the 56th General Assembly, he also served as the General Assembly's Presidential assistant.

The Ambassador outlined that the July 2009 North Korean nuclear test is the most pressing issue facing the Security Council. The passage of Resolution 1874 of the Security Council expresses its gravest concern that the nuclear test and missile activities carried out by the Democratic People's Republic of Korea have further generated increased tension in the region and beyond. Determining that there continues to exist a clear threat to international peace and security encourages UN Member States to search North Korean cargo in the aftermath of an underground nuclear test conducted May 25, 2009.

While there are approximately fifty million in South Korea and twenty-three million in North Korea, Ambassador Kim emphasized that to understand the Korean peninsula an important element must be understood. First and foremost, the Korean society has been based on Confucianism for more than 800 years. As a Confucian Society all Koreans are instilled with a strong loyalty to country, respect for elders, faithfulness, and obedience to family.

The Ambassador also emphasized that South Korea, with an economy the size of Brazil or India, is the world's leader in shipbuilding, a leading country for computer and automobile production, and ranks about thirty in contributing to the support of the United Nations. While it contributes about $1 billion to the MDGs (UN Millennium Development Goals), it plans to increase its donations to $2 billion in 2012, and $3 billion in assistance by 2015.

North Korea on the other hand is reliant on food aid and earns most of its hard currency from selling military and weapon systems to Iraq and Syria.

The other issues for the future are that Kim's oldest son is living outside of North Korea, and Kim is grooming his third son to replace him in light of his poor health. Reports that Kim Jong Il suffered a stroke in mid-August heightened speculation about a successor.

Kim will hand leadership over to his third son, Swiss-educated Kim Jong Un, who is in his midtwenties, passing power to a third son is not customary and may not be considered ligament to North Korean citizens.

However, the possibly of a collapsed state is also a huge concern of China because they would have to curtail a huge number of refuges crossing over the China border. China and Russia, as neighbors of North Korea, were very affected by the possible pollution of this testing, and both have joined in the resolution. There are still 30,000 United States Troops stationed on the border.

Mission of Uzbekistan, H.E. Murad Askarov

Mission of Uzbekistan, H.E. Murad Askarov, spoke to the United Nations about Uzbekistan's Political and Economic situation and the activities of the Mission of Uzbekistan. Information obtained from the US State Department indicates that Uzbekistan is Central Asia's most populous country. Its 28 million people, concentrated in the south and east of the country, are nearly half the region's total population. Uzbekistan had been one of the least developed republics of the Soviet Union; much of its population was engaged in cotton farming in small rural communities. The population continues to be heavily rural and dependent on farming for its livelihood.

The economy is based primarily on agriculture and natural resource extraction. Uzbekistan is a major producer and exporter of cotton, but natural gas has replaced it as the dominant source of foreign currency earnings. It also is a major exporter of gold, uranium, and strategic minerals (Uranium is Uzbekistan's largest export to the United States). Manufacturing has become increasingly important, particularly in the automotive sector, which is aimed primarily at exporting to the Russian market. Since independence, the government has followed a policy of gradual transition to a free market economy but most large enterprises are still state owned or controlled.

Holy See Permanent Observer, Archbishop Francis Assisi Chullikatt

Archbishop Francis Assisi Chullikatt was appointed on July 17, 2010 by Pope Benedict XVI as the Vatican's top envoy at the UN. Born in India, Archbishop Chullikatt is the Holy See Permanent Observer at the UN, replacing Archbishop Celestino Migliore, who last month was named the

Vatican's Apostolic Nuncio to Poland. The Vatican was granted the status of Nonvoting Permanent Observer State at the UN in 1964 under Pope Paul VI by an invitation from Secretary-General U Thant.

Archbishop Chullikatt is the first non-Italian to head the Holy See's Mission in New York. In addition to his native language, Malayalam, the archbishop is fluent in English, Spanish, French, Italian, and Latin. Since 2006, he was assigned to the Middle East as the Apostolic Nuncio to war-torn Iraq and also Jordan. He has also served as a Vatican diplomat in Honduras, South Africa, and the Philippines at the Vatican Secretariat for Relations with the States—the Holy See's equivalent of a Foreign Ministry. From 2000 to 2004, he served as Counselor for the Holy See Mission to the UN in New York. He was ordained a priest in 1978 and holds a Doctorate in Canon Law and joined the Vatican's diplomatic service in 1988.

He is known for his outspoken defense of persecuted Christians and other religious minorities in Iraq, and for his work on interreligious cooperation and good relations with Muslim leaders. Terrorists frequently targeted Christians and churches in Iraq, as well as his residence several times.

Permanent Representative of the Republic of Kazakhstan, H.E. Ms. Byrganym Aitimova

Ambassador Aitimova has held various positions in the Kazakhstan Government such as Minister of Education, Ambassador to Italy, and Ambassador to Israel, and she held a senatorial seat in Parliament.

In the 1940s the Soviet Union detonated its first nuclear weapon at a test facility in northeast Kazakhstan known as the Semipalatinsk Polygon. There were more than 400 atomic explosions conducted until the test site closed in 1991. Residents were exposed to the effects of the testing, which devastated three generations of people in the area with health problems ranging from thyroid diseases, cancer, birth defects, deformities, premature aging, and cardiovascular diseases.

Ambassador of Botswana, H.E. Mr. Charles Thembani Ntwaagae

His topic was "Why is Botswana so Successful" and its role at the UN. Prior to his appointment, Mr. Ntwaagae was Permanent Secretary in Botswana's Ministry of Foreign Affairs and International Cooperation since 2006. From 2001 to 2005, he served as his country's Permanent Representative to the United Nations Office in Geneva with concurrent accreditation to Austria and Greece. Between 1996 and 2001, Mr. Ntwaagae was Deputy Permanent Secretary in the Foreign Ministry. Before assuming those responsibilities, he was Chief Executive at the National Secretariat of the National Conservation Strategy (Coordinating) Agency, charged with promoting conservation and sustainable utilization of Botswana's natural resource base.

From 1993 to 1995, he was appointed Deputy Permanent Secretary in the Ministry of Local Government, Lands, and Housing, having previously served as Acting Deputy Permanent Secretary in that Ministry since 1992. Mr. Ntwaagae has a master's degree from Pennsylvania University, and a bachelor's degree from the University of Botswana and Swaziland. Born in 1953, in Tutume, Botswana, he is married and has three children.

Brazilian Mission, Mr. Aloisio Barbosa De Sousa Neto

The Secretary joined the Ministry of External Relations of Brazil in 2007 after receiving a degree in International Relations at the University of Brasilia in 2006. He is currently very active in the First Committee of the General Assembly, which deals with Disarmament and International Security.

A founding member of the United Nations, Brazil has a long tradition of contributing to peacekeeping operations. Brazil has participated in thirty-three United Nations peacekeeping operations and contributed over 27,000 troops. Currently, Brazil contributes more than 2,200 troops, military observers, and police officers in three continents.

Brazil has led the military component of MINUSTAH (United Nations Stabilization Mission in Haiti) since its establishment in 2004. The Mission's Force Commander is Major General Fernando Rodrigues

Goulart of the Brazilian Army. Brazil is the biggest troop-contributing country to MINUSTAH with 2,200 active military personnel.

From the Wikipedia website:
https://en.wikipedia.org/wiki/Niter%C3%B3i-class_frigate)

Brazil also leads the MTF (Maritime Task Force) of the UNIFIL (United Nations Interim Force in Lebanon). Since February 2011, the UNIFIL MTF has been under the command of Rear Admiral Luiz Henrique Caroli of the Brazilian Navy. The Brazilian Navy Niterói-class frigate União, is the flagship of the fleet comprising vessels from three other countries.

Brazil is the tenth largest contributor to the United Nations regular budget, with a net contribution of US $38 million for the 2012 Assessment.

Permanent Observer of the Holy See, His Excellency, The Most Reverend Celestino Migliore

The following remarks made by His Excellency, The Most Reverend Celestino Migliore, Titular Archbishop of Canosa, Apostolic Nuncio, were part of a discussion that took place at the monthly International Breakfast Meeting of the International Service Division of the Rotary Club of New York. The meeting was held on June 16, 2004 at the German Permanent Mission to the United Nations in New York City. This is a condensed and edited text made available as a resource to update Rotarians on current issues facing the International Development Community. The meeting was opened and moderated by Mr. Sylvan M. Barnet.

MR. BARNET: Archbishop Migliore obtained his Master's Degree in Theology at the Center of Theological Studies in Fossano, and was awarded the Doctorate in Canon Law. In 1980 he joined the Holy See's diplomatic service. His first assignment was to Angola as Attaché and then as Second Secretary to the Apostolic Delegation of LGN (Logos Global Network) as Head of Delegation of the Holy Land from 1980 to 1984. From there, he was transferred to the Apostolic Nunciature in the United States of America where he served as First Secretary and Alternate Observer to the Organization of American States. In 1988 he was appointed to the Apostolic Nunciature in Egypt, remaining there for a year. He was then assigned as Counselor to the Apostolic Nunciature in Warsaw, Poland, a post he held until his appointment in 1992 as Special

Envoy with a role of Permanent Observer of the Holy See to the Council of Europe in Strasbourg, France.

From 1995 to 2002 he served as Undersecretary of the Section for Relations with States of the Secretariat of State at the Vatican. During his term, he was also in charge of fostering relations with several Asian countries that do not yet have formal diplomatic relations with the Holy See. In this capacity, he traveled to Beijing, Hanoi, and Pyongyang as Head of Delegation of the Holy See. For the past six years, he was also teaching Ecclesiastical Diplomacy at the Pontifical Lateran University in Rome as visiting Professor. On October 30, 2003, His Holiness Pope John Paul of the Holy See to the United Nations, nominated Archbishop Celestino Migliore as Apostolic Nuncio and Permanent Observer of the Holy See to the United Nations in New York.

His Excellency Archbishop Celestino Migliore: We speak today about the diplomacy of the Holy See. Diplomacy and Holy See—that seems to be a contradiction in terms. In fact, diplomacy is a work full of meaning. The popular notion is that, which is associated with Machiavelli, when he said: "Diplomacy is the art of getting what you want at any cost and by any means." Can the Holy See accept this concept of diplomacy?

We must first clear the ground of a common equivocation between the Holy See and the Vatican City State. The "Holy See" is the Pope, together with all the bodies of the Roman Curia through which he governs the Catholic Church. The Holy See is a sovereign juridical person because it is the supreme organ of the Catholic Church. Its attributes as a sovereign subject are recognized in international law. It is the Holy See, and not the Vatican that is the juridical interlocutor within the international community.

In 1929, the Vatican State was created by the agreement between the Holy See and the Kingdom of Italy. They decided to establish Vatican City in order to assure the Pope a basis for his absolute independence and autonomy from any earthly power. The Vatican is intended only to ensure independence for the action of the Holy See, thanks to a territorial sovereignty reduced to its minimal expression.

The Vatican does not pursue the aims that are proper to a country, which has to guarantee the political, social, and economic rights of its population. The diplomacy of the Holy See does not lie upon military might or economic strength. Rather, the Holy See participated in diplomacy to have its voice heard within the international community. It is interested in following and participating in the work of the UN more so from its perspective as a world stage rather than as a center of global governance. Therefore, the diplomacy of the Holy See has characteristics, which are different from those of the countries of the world.

One needs to remember that fundamental principle of international law according to which every subject exercises its rights and the proper competence on relation to its nature and interests. It is for this reason that the activity of the Holy See remains concentrated in a certain order of rapport well-defined in relation to its nature and end.

When one says that the nature and mission of the Holy See are chiefly of a spiritual order, it follows that its activities tend to highlight a particular vision of a person and therefore, of human society that is not separated from the transcendence. It is this conviction that has a clear impact on every justice, peace and war, coexistence among peoples, and religious liberty.

The universal nature of the Holy See, which does not know national borders, allows the Holy See to be committed not only to hot topics on the international scene, but on all critical situations. And I would like to say, in particular on those, which are more easily forgotten or overlooked because they lack economic, political, or strategic interests, but especially on human persons, as in concentric circles that extend for the human person to the first communities, which are the family, school, work, social places, up to the local and national communities, and then to the international setting. In sum, these are the specific guidelines of the diplomacy of the Holy See: a precise and distinct anthropological vision, universality and ethical and humanitarian interests. Perhaps we can better capture these specific facets of the diplomacy of the Holy See with the aid of some examples.

Last week, the mass media in commemorating the special contribution of the late President Regan to the fall of the Soviet bloc, also mentioned in passing the contribution of Pope John Paul II. Well, if we look back carefully to what Pope John Paul II did, we find that his entire contribution stems from the specific and distinct anthropological vision mentioned above.

The Soviet Regime intended to reach a communist globalization. Communism was based on the premise that social class struggle, the real engine of history, would sooner or later result in the solidification of the communist society all over the world. The tenets of its strategy were namely, the prevalence of collective society on the individual human being and consequently, the deferral of individual human rights and freedoms to the collective interests. The means to teach a Communist society was basically class struggle, which in the end means mutual mistrust, and even hatred. Specificities of national, cultural, and religious identities of the different peoples were considered superstructures, destined to disappear. In point of actual fact, they were diametrically opposed to the social doctrine of the Church, which is based on the assumption that solidarity and subsidiarity are the core rules of a globalized society. Both stem from fundamental principles of respect for the dignity of the human person.

The principle of subsidiarity maintains that nations, communities, ethnic or religious groups, families or individuals, should not be anonymously immersed into a large conglomeration, which will result in their loss of identity. The Catholic Church specifically developed the category of subsidiarity long ago in order to face the stifling regimes like Marxism, Nazism, Fascism, and several dictatorships.

A dozen years ago, certain European circles complained about the premature recognition by the Holy See of Slovenia and Croatia as autonomous republics, independent from the Yugoslavian confederation. Actually, this decision was grounded on a couple of objective reasons; namely, the need for self-defense against the federal army that Belgrade was employing to fight and crush its own confederation territories.

The decision stemmed above all, from the deep conviction of Pope John Paul II that those republics like any other republic coming from the socialist bloc, regardless of their territorial or demographic size, needed to be given the chance to regain their proper cultural, social, religious, and political identity. They needed to find in their own approach and sensitivity for human rights, and rule of law. It was only by becoming deeply-rooted in their own identity, which had been confiscated for so long by an imposed unification, that those countries would be able to join and make their own specific contribution to a larger economic, political or security system, or an association of countries. To affirm the necessity to protect the rights of peoples does not simply mean to give them a new subjectivity; rather, to discover and develop a new international order more responsive to the needs of all peoples.

In his second trip to Poland in 1983, John Paul II offered strong support to the newly born Solidarność movement, led by Lech Walesa. We could gather from his gestures, as well as from his message, that he did not intend to give a near, even if vital impetus, to the police, social, and humanitarian uprising in Poland. He saw a glimpse of the germination off a cultural revolution capable of allowing the maturation of a new societal organization, suitable not only for Poland but for the entire world.

And it is for this reason that he appealed to the Polish bishops and clergy exhorting them to take this opportunity to create a culture, and to attentively observe the phenomenon of Solidarność and to use that as a base upon which to develop a new vision of relation: human, civil, social, and international. The culture of solidarity as envisioned by John Paul II was a nonviolent approach, precisely because it substituted the battle of classes with solidarity, which intended to erode and eventually dismantle every unjust and evil aspect of the communist system. The conviction of John Paul II, however, was farsighted: he envisioned in the category of solidarity the possibility to construct a new world order after the fall of communism and the numerous insufficiencies and deficits of capitalism. Under the category of solidarity, society is organized upon rights and the need for individual and group participation; the distribution of goods and riches will no longer be solely according to the availability of resources, but also in light of the equal dignity of every human person.

So, when the Holy See speaks of global governments in terms of global solidarity, it freely uses the motto, "Let's globalize solidarity," by which it refers not simply to acts of solidarity nor to generic humanitarian perspective, but to a solid long-lasting culture, social, economic, and political project which encompasses each and every concentric circle of human society.

In the context of the Cold War there was a prevalent political vision, of then ideological, regarding social realities, economies, cultures, and religions. The fall of Communism has contributed to the development of market law. Speaking of the common economy in a globalized context is equivalent to thinking of a social system revolving around the daily lives of thousands and millions of people.

The Holy See has become particularly attentive to the economy. The Pope has dedicated three great encyclicals: *Laborem Exercens, Sollicitudo Rei Socialis,* and *Centesimus Annus*, other than the post-synodal apostolic exhortations to the churches in Africa, America, and Europe, and some programmatic discourses on globalization, directed in an article to the Pontifical Academy of Sciences. In 1998, the Holy See adopted the status of Permanent Observer at the World Trade Organization closely monitoring the world conference of Geneva, Seattle, Doha, and Cancun. In the context of the United Nations Organization, the Holy See has taken part in the conference at Monterrey on financing for development.

"The Role of the Holy See and Catholic Organizations at the United Nations" *By Josef Klee, PhD*

June 29, 2017

The Holy See as the "Government" of the Catholic Church, as well as the international Catholic organizations are strong supporters of the UN (United Nations Organization) and actively participate in the deliberations and activities of this world body.

The scope and the nature of the involvement of the Holy See and the Catholic organizations in the work of the United Nations is determined by the mandates and the programs carried out by the UN Organization.

As a worldwide organization with a unique global mission, the Charter of the United Nations outlines the four major goals and areas of its programs and activities, namely:

1. Maintenance of Peace and Security
2. Protection of Human Rights
3. Development of International Law
4. Advancement of Economic and Social Progress

In accordance with these overall goals and the related needs of the world community, the United Nations and its subsidiary organizations have undertaken activities in various global fields, such as: international disputes, economic and social development, commerce and trade law, human rights, migration, peacekeeping, humanitarian assistance, health services, protection of the environment, as well as the technical coordination of international air, postal, and communications services, the registration of international patent rights, and the classification of drugs and chemicals, etc.

An indication of the heavy UN workload is the extensive number of agenda items reviewed and debated yearly by the UN General Assembly. This year, the General Assembly will address 135 main agenda items, which regularly include a number of sub-items on the execution of related matters.

In order to carry out the diverse mandates and functions, the UN since its inception, has gradually established a large number of specialized organizational entities which now comprise the so called United Nations Family of Organizations.

The copy of the organizational chart, added at the end of this paper, provides a respective overview of the many legislative bodies, administrative, and operational entities of the United Nations System. It particularly shows that the UN has experienced a dramatic increase in peacekeeping operations since 1990. Today, the UN manages 15 peacekeeping missions with a total number of more than 110,000 personnel consisting of 95,000 military and police forces and 15,000 civilian support staff while the annual peacekeeping budget has reached more than $8 billion.

NOTE: The UN is often blamed for not being able to resolve an international political crisis and for being a very costly and ineffective bureaucratic organization. Some of the criticism is justified. However, one should be fair and acknowledge that the political decisions at the UN are exclusively taken by its Member States; and if these do not agree on certain issues—as often is the case—the United Nations Secretary-General and his staff cannot act without the absolute authority and consent of the legislative bodies such as the General Assembly or the Security Council.

Likewise, the considerable expansion of UN mandates and activities over the years has also become a challenge for the Holy See and the Catholic organizations, which are faced with a substantial increase in their efforts to respond to this expansion.

At the UN, the Catholic Church is accredited under the historical diplomatic designation "Holy See" and not as often assumed under the title "Vatican." However, the content and designation of both terms are based on the historical and judicial developments of the Catholic Church. As such, the "Holy See" is the universal government of the Catholic Church with its headquarters located in "Vatican City."

The word, "See," used in the term "Holy See" is derived from the Latin word "sedes" and embodies the "seat of St. Peter." The Holy See as the seat of St. Peter has a history of 2000 years; and the denomination "Holy See" refers not only to the Pope in his position as the "head of church," but also to the Roman Curia and thus to the central governance of the Catholic Church.

Since the time of King Charles the Great (742-814) and during the Middle Ages until the creation of the Italian State in the year 1870, the Holy See enjoyed the status and privileges of a sovereign state. It maintained a diplomatic corps to take care of the worldly interest of the so-called Papal States and the ecclesial responsibilities for the Catholic Church.

In 1929 the Italian Government and the Holy See signed the Lateran Treaty, which formally recognizes the independence of Vatican City and the Holy See as a sovereign international judicial entity. It is interesting to note that earlier in 1908, the United States Supreme Court recognized the Holy See as an entity in international law.

Only in 1964, the Holy See received an official status with the United Nations as a so-called "Permanent Observer State." It was UN Secretary-General U Thant, a Buddhist from Burma (Myanmar), who invited the Holy See to join the United Nations and participate in its work. However, earlier the Holy See had already joined either as a member (similar to regular Member States) or as an observer to some of the older UN subsidiary organizations, such as the UN Postal Union or the World Health Organization.

It is interesting to note that in 1964 the Holy See maintained diplomatic relations with 38 countries of the then 115 UN Member States; and today the Holy See has full diplomatic relations with 182 of the current 193 UN Member States. Accordingly, the Holy See maintains one of the world's most extensive diplomatic networks.

Throughout the history of the Catholic Church, the Popes have carried out the role of peacemakers and they have promoted and assisted in finding peaceful solutions to international conflicts.

Since attaining its observer status, the Popes have expressed their high esteem and support for the United Nations Organization by their visits to the United Nations. Pope Paul VI was the first visitor in October 1965, Pope Paul II twice visited the UN in 1979 and in 1995, Pope Benedict XVI in 2008, and Pope Francis in 2015.

Pope Paul VI in his speech to the General Assembly stated that the purpose of his visit was to be, "first of all, a moral and solemn ratification of this lofty institution. The edifice that you have constructed must never collapse. It must be continually perfected and adopted to the needs that the history of the world will present."

In October 1979, Pope John Paul II in his statement to the UN General Assembly, said: "As a universal community embracing faithful belonging to almost all countries and continents, nations, peoples, races, languages, and cultures, the Church is deeply interested in the existence and activity of the organization whose name tells us that it unites and associates nations.

Pope Francis in his address to the General Assembly, reiterated the appreciation expressed by his predecessors and he reaffirmed, "the importance that the Catholic Church attaches to this institution and the hope that she placed in its activities."

But he also voiced some concern with regard to the full application of international norms and the lack of enforcement.

The Holy See's role at the United Nations is different from other Member States. Archbishop Migliore, the former Nuncio in New York, describes the presence of the Holy See at the United Nations as follows: "The Holy See acts in the international arena according to its nature and ends, which are essentially religious, moral, and humanitarian. The religious nature of the Holy See means that it considers vital the creative impact of religious and ethical factors capable of influencing the evolution of geopolitical paradigms."

The involvement of the Holy See at the United Nations routinely consists of coverage of all UN agenda items, but with emphasis on priority areas which include:

- Protection and promotion of the dignity of the human person and the traditional family
- Promotion of peace and peaceful settlements of international disputes
- Disarmament
- Protection of human rights and in particular, the protection of religious freedom
- Alleviation of poverty
- Economic and social development and humanitarian assistance

The Holy See is also a strong supporter of the International Criminal Court established in 1998 to prosecute individuals who commit genocide, war crimes, and crimes against humanity.

Recently, in his speech at Seton Hall University, the present Nuncio of the New York Mission to the United Nations, Archbishop B. Auza, has outlined the principles that guide Pope Francis in the diplomatic activities of the Holy See, stating, "It is a diplomacy of dialogue to resolve conflicts, to promote unity and fight exclusion. This is a diplomacy that privileges greater respect for the weaker countries, the rule of law over the law of force, honest and cordial relations among nations and peoples over mutual suspicions."

Following this lead of Pope Francis, the Holy See has identified specific priority areas for 2017:

- Ceaseless pursuit of peace, in particular, in war-torn areas (In the last decade, the number of conflicts has increased from 13 to 39 in 2016.)
- Pursuit of disarmament, in particular, abolition of nuclear arms
- Protection and assistance of refugees, migrants and internally displaced people across the globe
- Fighting human trafficking and other forms of modern slavery eradication of extreme poverty
- Defense and promotion of the dignity of every person and of the family

The Holy See maintains three diplomatic offices accredited within the United Nations, namely in New York, Geneva, and Vienna. These offices are under the leadership of a Nuncio (Ambassador) and perform typical diplomatic functions similar to those of an ambassador of a regular UN Member State Mission. In addition, the Holy See has appointed representatives at a number of UN bodies, which are not located in New York, Geneva, or Vienna.

The Holy See Mission in New York employs three priest diplomats, two priests on secondment from US dioceses, more than two dozen lay volunteer experts (advisors) and a number of office and household staff. The Nuncio, his staff and the advisors follow closely the debates in the various legislative bodies of the UN; and, if deemed necessary, will take the floor and make official statements for the Holy See, presenting the views and special concerns of the Church regarding the particular issue in question.

There are critics who question the presence and role of the Holy See at the United Nations. These critics claim that the Holy See is nothing more than any other NGO (nongovernmental organization) such as all the other religious groups and churches admitted to the UN as NGOs, while the Holy See is awarded preferential treatment similar to that of a regular UN Member State.

Several years ago, critics tried to ouster the Holy See as an Observer State from the UN. In response to such attacks, UN Member States as friends of the Holy See, introduced a General Assembly resolution in 2004 to reconfirm and strengthen the role and participation of the Holy See in the work of the United Nations. The General Assembly adopted this resolution without any reservations.

The text of the resolution highlights the fact that the Holy See is party to numerous UN treaties and conventions and that the Holy See enjoys membership in many UN subsidiary bodies and agencies. It also mentions that the Holy See pays the regular established annual contribution to the UN budget for financing of the United Nations programs.

Furthermore, the key paragraph of the resolution states: "the Holy See, in its capacity as an Observer State, shall be accorded the rights and privileges of participation in the sessions and work of the General Assembly and international conferences."

The adoption of this resolution was a great success for the Holy See, and it demonstrates the high esteem the Holy See enjoys within the community of United Nations Member States.

In general, outsiders often do not know that NGOs, including many Catholic lay organizations and religious orders, can have an official affiliation with the United Nations. Presently, 4.500 NGOs of diverse backgrounds and expertise enjoy an active consultative status with the UN Economic and Social Council, and 1.500 NGOs have an association with the UN Department of Public Information.

NOTE: Since the inception of the United Nations in 1945, Rotary International has been a strong supporter of the United Nations and has established an official affiliation with the UN Economic and Social Council. Rotary International enjoys, within the UN community, a unique reputation for its strong support and its effective leadership in so many development and humanitarian assistance projects, and in particular, for its Polio eradication campaign.

NGOs operate either as advocates in certain fields, such as human rights or the protection of the environment, or they provide operational support services in various humanitarian or development areas. Among these NGOs are many Catholic organizations which are strong supporters of the United Nations. They also play an active role within the NGO community itself, and they enjoy an excellent reputation internationally.

Historically, already ninety years ago, Catholic organizations have been affiliated with the predecessor of the United Nations—the League of Nations—and they have been involved from the outset in the work of many early international organizations which now belong to the UN System.

Some of the Catholic organizations participated in the San Francisco Charter Conference for the establishment of the United Nations, and they were instrumental in drafting the composition of Article 79 of the UN Charter which recognizes the participation of NGOs in the work of the UN.

More than 30 Catholic organizations have an affiliation with the United Nations in New York, either with the UN Department of Economic and Social Affairs or with the UN Department of Public Information.

The main purpose of these Catholic NGOs is the promotion of Catholic social principles and values, such as peace, social justice, compassion, tolerance, and solidarity.

Catholic NGOs also operate as advocates for a special international cause; for example, Pax Christi and Pax Romana are strong advocates for disarmament, the peaceful settlements of disputes, and for the protection of human rights. Other Catholic organizations provide humanitarian relief and other operational assistance services in developing countries; prominently among them are the Knights of Malta, Caritas Internationalis, and the Community of Sant'Egidio.

The Sovereign Order of Malta (with its full official title of "Sovereign Military Hospitaller Order of St. John of Jerusalem, of Rhodes, and of Malta") is an international Catholic organization with a long and prestigious history (founded in 1048 in Jerusalem, to tend to sick pilgrims arriving in the Holy Land).

NOTE: Today, the Order is recognized as a sovereign subject of international law and thus maintains diplomatic relations with 106 states. At the UN, the Order is recognized as a special entity with an official observer status, and the head of the office in New York carries the title "Ambassador and Permanent Observer."

The core missions, or "charismas" of the Order of Malta are to defend the Catholic faith (Tuitio Fidei) and to serve the poor and the sick (Obsequium Pauperum). The Order counts more than 13,500 members—"Knights and Dames"—and provides a variety of services to the poor worldwide, with emphasis on providing medical care, including emergency situations. The Order employs 25,000 professional and support staff, which are assisted by 80,000 volunteers in more than 120 countries. Its annual budget is about 200 million Euros.

Even though the central "government" of the Order of Malta is headquartered in Rome, the works of the Order are carried out on a much decentralized basis, with responsibility for service activities falling on 47 "national associations" scattered throughout the world.

NOTE: The adjective "military" derives from the fact that the Order of Malta was forced to adopt a military character, mostly for reasons of self-defense and to protect its activities in the Holy Land. This need for defense continued while the Order was headquartered in Rhodes (14th and 15th centuries) and later in Malta (16th, 17th and 18th centuries) because of continued aggression from the Ottoman Empire.

The Order of Malta takes a strong interest in the activities of the United Nations, particularly those that fall under the humanitarian and human rights domains. It has been an active participant in discussions leading to better coordination of humanitarian efforts, the adoption of global agreements on the treatment of refugees and migrants, and the fight against the trafficking in persons. It is also very concerned with the widespread disregard for international humanitarian law, particularly the plight of innocent civilians in situations of armed conflict.

Caritas Internationalis consists of a large international Catholic humanitarian and relief services confederation with 165 member organizations in all regions of the world. Caritas was established in 1897 in Germany to serve the poor and needy of the population. Today, Caritas Internationalis organizations provide humanitarian, social, and economic development assistance, as well as relief and emergency services in more than 200 countries and territories worldwide.

At the United Nations Headquarters in New York, Caritas Internationalis maintains a Liaison Office with the objective to advocate on all international issues related to social justice, and to interact with United Nations Organizations in order to coordinate Caritas Internationalis projects with United Nations mandates and programs worldwide.

The 165 national Caritas Internationalis organizations provide a variety of services to the poor and needy in their own countries; in addition, many of them carry out humanitarian, relief and other assistance services in developing countries. For example, Caritas Germany, the oldest and largest Caritas Internationalis organization, operates as an established national welfare association providing services on health care and social care, as well as on education and employment. Next to the German Government, Caritas Germany is the largest employer with a workforce of more than 600.000 in numerous branch offices and facilities, and the regular staff is supported by half a million volunteers.

Caritas Germany maintains an international department which is in charge of 650 projects in developing countries implementing health, humanitarian, economic assistance, relief, and emergency programs.

The Community of Sant'Egidio is an international Catholic lay organization founded in Rome in 1968 by Andrea Riccardi with members in more than seventy countries. It is recognized by the Holy See as a Public Lay Association. Its main mission is to spread the gospel, to serve the poor and to promote dialogue among religions.

The community is renowned for its successful peace mediation in the Mozambican war and in other conflict zones. Among them: Algeria, 1994-1995; Guatemala, 1996; Albania, 1997; Kosovo, 1996-1998; Burundi, 1998-2000; Bosnia, 2001 Liberia: 2003-2004; Cote d'Ivoire, 2002-2004; Togo, 2004-2005; Darfur, 2005; North Uganda, July 2006-2008; Cote d'Ivoire, April 2010; Guinea Conakry, June 2010; Niger, October 2010; Libya, since January 2011; and Senegal–Casamance, since 2012. Most recently the Community of Sant'Egidio, which has been present in the Central African Republic since 2003, facilitated the reconciliation process that led to the signature of the Republican Pact (September 2013) and more recently, the agreement for immediate cease-fire and a road map to peace.

The Community of Saint'Egidio has been active in the United Nations system since the '90s when regular contacts for the Mozambique peace process were established. It has consultative status with ECOSOC (Economic and Social Council). In 2017 the Community of Sant'Egidio signed an agreement in the form of an exchange of letters with the DPA (Department of Political Affairs) to strengthen the collaboration on conflict resolution, peacebuilding initiatives and political dialogue in areas of crisis. The President of the Community of Sant'Egidio briefed the Security Council on the situation in CAR (Central African Republic) on June 12, 2017 prior to the agreement signed in Rome.

Overall, the work of the Holy See and the Catholic Organizations at the United Nations is truly impressive. I wish the Church would do a better job of informing its parishioners about its valuable contribution to the international community.

In light of the many political, economic, and social changes in the world during the last decades, the United Nations Secretariat and its many subsidiary organizations must undertake reforms and adjustments in order to be able to meet today's global challenges and instill credibility among all nations. In spite of its shortcomings and inefficiencies the United Nations is a unique global institution striving to maintain peace and security in the world, and seeking to serve as a forum to address global issues no single country or region can resolve alone. In my view, the United Nations deserves the support of the Catholic Church in all parts of the world.

Permanent Representative of Sierra Leone, H.E. Joe Robert Pemagbi

H.E. Joe Robert Pemagbi, the Permanent Representative of Sierra Leone to the United Nations, met with Rotarians for an informal breakfast meeting to review a variety of democratic and economic issues facing Sierra Leone, and humanitarian projects Rotary is conducting in Africa.

From 1999 until his current appointment, Ambassador Pemagbi was Chairman of the National Commission for Democracy and Human Rights in Sierra Leone, and a member of the Commission since 1994, where his duties included formulating and raising awareness about democracy, civic rights and responsibilities, and human rights. He received his Master's Degree in Linguistics from the University of Leeds (1976) and his Bachelor's Degree in Education from the University of Sierra Leone in 1972.

Sierra Leone became an independent nation from Britain on April 27, 1961. A military coup overthrew the civilian government in 1967, which was in turn replaced by civilian rule a year later. The country declared itself a republic on April 19, 1971.

The Sierra Leone Civil War began in 1991, initiated by the RUF (Revolutionary United Front). Tens of thousands died and more than 2 million people (well over one-third of the population) were displaced because of the nine-year conflict. Neighboring countries became host to significant numbers of refugees attempting to escape the civil war. It was officially declared over on January 18, 2002.

Considered one of the world's poorest countries, Sierra Leone has been ranked last by the HDI (United Nations Human Development Index) for 2007-08.

The HDI is a comparative measure of life expectancy, literacy, education, and standards of living for countries worldwide. It is a standard means of measuring well-being, especially child welfare. It is used to distinguish whether the country is a developed, a developing, or an underdeveloped country and also to measure the impact of economic policies on quality of life.

About two-thirds of the population engages in subsistence agriculture, which accounts for 52% of national income. The government is trying to increase food and cash-crop production and upgrade small farmer skills. Also, the government works with several foreign donors to operate integrated rural development and agricultural projects.

According to the US State Department, Sierra Leone is rich in minerals and has relied on the mining sector in general, and diamonds in particular, for its economic base. By the 1990s economic activity was declining and economic infrastructure had become seriously degraded. Over the next decade much of Sierra Leone's formal economy was destroyed in the country's civil war. Since the cessation of hostilities in January 2002, massive infusions of outside assistance have helped Sierra Leone begin to recover. Full recovery to prewar economic levels will require hundreds of millions of additional dollars and many more years of serious effort by the Government of Sierra Leone and donor governments.

President of the 60th Session of the UN General Assembly, H.E. Mr. Jan Eliasson

President of the 60th Session of the UN General Assembly, Jan Eliasson, who is the senior ranking officer of the United Nations, addressed the Assembly. President Eliasson is the former Sweden Ambassador to the United States and Swedish Permanent Representative to the United Nations. Coincidently, President Eliasson is from the same town in Sweden as our own Rotary International President.

President Eliasson stated that he was a recipient of the Rotary High School Exchange Program and studied for one year in Indiana. During that time, he addressed more than 50 Rotary Clubs and one unforgettable Indiana Ladies Church group.

During his talk, he suggested that we must remember, "There is a world outside of Verona," as written in Shakespeare's *Romeo and Juliet*. To show that, "We must be engaged not only in our local and national scenes but also internationally. We need to reach the moment in history when we all understand that good and effective international cooperation is indeed in our national interest. The fact that we can say that we are truly internationalist confirms why we love our country. We all need to show the world that we have international solutions for international problems."

The Ambassador of El Salvador, Rubén Hasbún

The Ambassador of El Salvador, Rubén Hasbún, who asked to be called "Ruben," first thanked The New York Rotary-supported, Gift of Life Program. He went on to say that eleven beautiful Salvadoran children received the Gift of Life this week at Hospital Bloom in El Salvador thanks to their amazing medical teams and our wonderful sponsors: Rotary Club of Naples, Michael Grech Memorial Foundation; Digicel El Salvador; Rotary District 7190; Rotary Clubs of Latham, Delmar, Scotia, Schenectady, Rotterdam Sunrise, Glens Falls; Club Rotario Santa Tecla, and the Rotary Foundation.

Rubin is the Deputy Permanent Representative of El Salvador to the United Nations and before that post was Minister Counselor in charge of human rights and social affairs. He also held the post of International Civil Society based in Tokyo, Japan for seven years where he earned his Master of Arts Degree in International Politics at Aoyama University. Ruben is fluent in Japanese and four other languages besides his native Spanish.

On human rights, he also supported the presentation of the report of the Committee on Economic, Cultural and Social Rights, and hoped that the request for extra meeting time would be adopted by consensus. The rights of older persons were an issue of growing importance, he said, and noted the upcoming Conference on Aging in that respect. As the report on that matter pointed out, the aging of the population was one of the most important changes in global demographics in the twenty-first century.

Lastly, on the issue of the Permanent Forum on Indigenous Issues, he said that his delegation attached great importance to the resolution adopted this year by the CEDAW (Committee on the Elimination of Discrimination Against Women) regarding indigenous women. El Salvador would continue to play an active role in the facilitation process of an inclusive draft resolution on the preparation of the 2014 World Conference on Indigenous Peoples.

Ambassador of Poland, Witold Sobków, Outlines WMD (Weapons of Mass Destruction) Policy

Ambassador Witold Sobków of Poland accepted our invitation to join our local business community at the monthly International Breakfast Meeting. As Permanent Representative at the UN since 2010, he sits on several committees and has played a key role in the strategy and planning of Poland's foreign policy. Early in his career, he spent years lecturing at Warsaw University and more recently he enjoyed a stint as the Polish Ambassador to Ireland.

In May of 2011, in New York, the Permanent Missions of Japan, Poland, and Turkey, in cooperation with the Washington-based think tank, "The Stimson Center" organized a seminar on promotion of WMD-related nonproliferation measures in the context of relevant activities undertaken within United Nations and following commitments resulting from the relevant Security Council resolutions. The UN Secretary-General, Mr. Ban Ki-moon, addressed the seminar.

Ambassador of Iraq, H.E. Samir Shakir Mahmood Sumaida'ie Outlines Iraq after First Election

Ambassador Samir Shakir Mahmood Sumaida'ie was trained as an engineer and studied in Iraq and the UK. He has had an extensive private sector business career, working for several international companies before starting his own company. He was an active political leader to fight the Saddam Hussein regime. He participated in numerous international conferences on the opposition movement, and in 2003 he became a member of the Governing Council of Iraq. In 2004, he was appointed as Minister of Interior Affairs. On Sept 15, 2004 he was appointed as Permanent Representative of Iraq to the UN.

The Ambassador described Baghdad of the late 1930s, when he was a boy. Life was gentle, steady, predictable, and his country had the best educational system in the region. As early as the 1930s, Iraq had a woman foreign minister and women were graduating with university degrees. Socially, the country was moving forward. However, during the 1950s, the country had taken a turn for the worst. The Royal Family was removed and military rule was imposed in 1958. Nonelected government officials dictating to those governed ensued, and human liberties were restricted. In 1968, the Saddam era began. Under his rule, Iraq transformed as the "most authoritarian regime" in the region. Economic activity plummeted and many Iraqi citizens were traumatized while educational opportunities diminished.

For decades, the opposition in exile labored to have Saddam Hussein removed. They lobbied the United States, the United Kingdom, as well as other counties for assistance. It was their view that without external intervention there was no hope to remove Saddam. The Ambassador stated that he is well aware of the controversy the intervention caused in the world community, especially in Europe. But he metaphorically stated that there was no choice: "Iraq was like a sore. It had to be lanced, and it had to be cleansed."

Since the removal of Saddam Hussein, Iraqi society has been adjusting from being "hermetically sealed" for decades. It had been highly traumatized and brutalized, and a culture of violence pervaded. While there is an overlap of insurgency and ordinary criminal activity, some Iraqis continued the pervasive culture of violence, mainly by those who lost their position and privileges. These insurgents are not accepting liberation, despite the fact that the bulk of the citizens are relieved. It is a law of nature that these "convulsions of adjustment" will gradually be diminished. In time, with the maturation of the political process and the help of the international community, tension will ease and Iraq will be nursed back to health, he emphasized. It is his view that the long-term prospect is positive, despite the extreme difficulty. He openly stated that the gentle and secure Baghdad of his youth is currently, in many areas, a desolate and dangerous place. But despite this—as proven by the Iraqis who went out to vote and to say to the world "we are here"—resilience, spirit, and backbone will defeat the reactionary forces. Over the longtime scale, Iraq will move in the right direction.

He pointed out that part of his job here in New York is to make sure that the international community does not lose its focus and continues its support for rebuilding Iraq. His country has to "face all the phantoms" that were released, but with the determination of the Iraqi people along with the assistance and understanding of the outside world, Iraq will prosper, he concluded.

Ambassador of South Korea, Sul Kyung-Hoon

Ambassador of South Korea, Sul entered the Ministry of Foreign Affairs and Trade in 1982. Since then, he has worked on a variety of multilateral issues related to economic and development cooperation, the United Nations, international economic organizations, disarmament and nonproliferation, and international law. He has assumed political, economic and consular posts in New York (1987-1990), Iran (1994-1996), Geneva (1998-2001), and Kuwait (2004-2006). From 2006 to 2009, he was posted as Minister-Counsellor at the Korean Mission to the United Nations in New York. He served as Deputy Director-General for International Organizations in 2009 and as Director-General for Development Cooperation dealing with development assistance to developing countries from 2009 to 2011. He began his post as Deputy Permanent Representative to the UN in August 2011.

Ambassador Sul received his Master of Arts in International Political Economy from the University of Virginia (1985). He received a Bachelor's Degree in Economics from Seoul National University (1981). In 2005, the Korean Government awarded him the red stripe medal for distinguished officials.

Consul General of Bulgaria, H.E. Mr. Milen Lyutskonov

Consul General of Bulgaria, H.E. Mr. Milen Lyutskonov, spoke about Central Europe and the Crimea from a Bulgarian Perspective.

Milen Lyutskanov, was appointed to represent his country in New York. He is a career diplomat with extensive service. Before his current post in New York, Milen Lyutskanov was Deputy Permanent Representative and Deputy Chief of the Bulgarian Mission to NATO. Mr. Lyutskanov was also Deputy Foreign Minister.

The President of Bulgaria, Rosen Plevneliev, is following with concern the development of the situation in Ukraine after Russia's Upper House of Parliament adopted a decree which allows the use of Russian armed forces in the Autonomous Republic of Crimea.

The Head of State has said more than once that the only lasting solution may be achieved by peaceful means and if the territorial integrity and sovereignty of Ukraine is guaranteed. The use of military force to occupy foreign territories is a violation of the rules of international law.

The President calls on the UN Security Council and the country's-guarantors of the security in Ukraine, in compliance with the Budapest Memorandum of 1994, to ensure a peaceful solution to the problem and to avoid a further escalation of the tension.

In May 2014, presidential elections are due to be held in Ukraine. The people of Ukraine should alone decide what their future should be in a democratic way. If necessary, the President will convene the Consultative Council for National Security.

China's Ambassador Zhanga Explains China's Role at the UN

Ambassador Yishan Zhang was the guest speaker at the International Breakfast Meeting of the Rotary Club of New York. He gave an enlightening and insightful summary of the economic advances and challenges of China, as well as providing the Chinese perspective of recent developments at the United Nations.

The meeting was hosted and moderated by New York Rotarian, Ambassador Wolfgang Trautwein of Germany. Ambassador Trautwein informed the participants that proceeds from the meeting were being donated to the new Rotary Club in Shanghai to help finance a health project and to foster a New York and Shanghai relationship. Alas, our host for the last two years also announced that he is likely to be assigned to a new position in Europe and will be leaving New York in July. The Ambassadors' friendship flourished while they were working together when Germany was a nonpermanent member of the Security Council and Ambassador Zhang was the Council's president at the beginning of the Iraq War.

China's Ambassador Zhanga explains China's Role and the UN. He is a graduate of Beijing Foreign Studies University and received advanced degrees from Columbia and Princeton University. His extensive career with China's MFA (Ministry of Foreign Affairs) includes service in Geneva and Vienna in an Ambassadorial capacity with the UNIDO (United Nations Industrial Development Organization) and the IAEA (International Atomic Energy Agency).

In the first part of his presentation, the Ambassador noted that China has three special characteristics that everyone should keep in mind:

First, China has a very long history. Ancient China made great contributions to mankind. However, in 1840, starting with the Opium War with Great Britain, China was colonized by Western powers and suffered under this colonial system. Then, with the end of foreign occupation, the period from 1949 to the present is considered as the time for the "Rebirth of the Chinese Civilization."

Second, China has a huge potential market and has sustained close to a 9% growth rate over the last years. In fact, recently President Bush stated, when discussing Sino-American relations, that, "China needs twenty-five million new jobs every year to stay even. Yet, I rejoice when our country gained four million new jobs since 2003." The Ambassador noted therefore that employment is a major dilemma of China. He said, "We have a huge market but we need to create twenty-five million jobs a year. No matter how small a problem is, when it is multiplied by 1.3 billion it becomes a huge problem. Conversely, no matter what the Chinese economy achieves, when it is divided by 1.3 billion it is not enough." Even though China is the 4th largest economy in the world after Germany in terms of per capita income, China is posted at 111th!

He noted that during the last two decades, China has changed dramatically. The most basic change is the transformation from a demand economy to a market economy. There are no longer government planned production quotas. In the past, there was no private ownership of property. In the cities; property was "state owned" and in the rural areas it was "collective owned." Today, more than two-thirds of China's economic growth comes from the private sector.

Third, even with impressive economic gains, China still considers itself a developing country. This is particularly evident by the vast income-gap between those of the coastal cities and western China. However, progress is being made. The Millennium Development Goals of 2000 set-out to reduce the poverty in the world by half within fifteen years. Mr. Zhang was pleased to declare that China has already achieved this goal. In 2000, China had 250 million of its citizens living below the poverty level. Today, it is less than 26 million. The ambassador noted that China has become polio-free with some assistance from Rotary's PolioPlus Program. However, there are about 600,000 HIV/AIDS victims in China, and the government is taking bold steps to reduce this rate.

China views the United Nations as the most universally represented, intergovernmental organization in the world, and therefore promotion of the United Nations is part of China's foreign policy.

He outlines the three pillars of the United Nations:

Security and Peace

Until recently, mainly because of its experience with colonialism, China has not favored the peacekeeping operations of the United Nations. However, it has changed its position gradually and now supports limited peacekeeping missions. Currently, China has some 6,000 civilian and armed personnel in several of the fifteen or so UN Peacekeeping Missions around the world.

Economic and Humanitarian Development

As a developing country and a member of the Group of 77, China feels developmental issues need more emphasis at the UN. China is working for trade regulation improvements between developing countries and developed economies because many countries have become poorer over the last twenty years.

Human Rights

The newly created Human Rights Council that replaced the often discredited Human Rights Commission will bring a "new page to the promotion and protection of human rights around the world." The Council has declared in its charter that the "Protection of Human Rights is the Responsibility of the State." Currently the Council is part of the General Assembly, but in five years its organizational effectiveness will be examined and it may then become a charter organization or remain under the General Assembly.

History of Rotary in China

Rotary has had a long, rich history with China. The first Rotary Club in Shanghai was chartered in 1919. By 1947 there were 32 clubs welcoming local businessmen and expatriates, but political changes resulted in the closure of all Rotary Clubs on mainland China by 1953.

Rotary leaders met with Chinese officials to introduce Rotary as early as 1982. Actively pursuing the possibilities of reintroducing Rotary to China, the RI (Rotary International) president led delegations to China in 2000 and 2002. The Board recognized that the Hong Kong Rotary Clubs became part of the People's Republic of China in 1999.
To demonstrate Rotary's humanitarian ideals, grants and exchanges have been encouraged. As part of PolioPlus, Rotary has given $22 million to eliminate polio in China—a milestone that was achieved in 2001. A total of seven Group Study Exchanges have occurred since 1991. In addition, starting in 1997, Rotary Clubs and the Rotary Foundation have built credibility by funding $975,000 in humanitarian projects throughout China, and Hong Kong clubs are raising US $1.3 million for Hepatitis B immunization for 1 million babies.

Provisional Rotary Clubs in China

Rotary International granted provisional status to clubs in Beijing and Shanghai in 2001 and appointed a Rotary International advisor to provide orientation to the club members. Currently, District 3450 provides training and support to the provisional clubs with the help of the three-year training subsidy from RI.

The 38 members of the Provisional Rotary Club of Shanghai achieved 100% Paul Harris Fellow status three years ago. Their major fundraising supports the Gift of Life Program, providing heart surgeries to Chinese children. They will participate in a GSE (Government-sponsored Enterprise) with District 5879 in Texas this year. In addition, the club administrators' three Matching Grants include a water project and a microcredit program to help women start businesses, and scholarship sponsorships to the Royal Melbourne Institute of Technology. Nine countries are represented in the club membership, primarily from Europe, North America, and Australia. Member classifications include medical consultant, professor, architect, lawyer, and business manager.

The Provisional Rotary Club of Beijing currently has five Matching Grants—the maximum number allowed. Four of the Matching Grants are designated for Gift of Life, including video conferencing between Chinese and US heart surgeons. More applications are pending, including a 3H grant. A Group Study Exchange with District 6490 in Illinois is planned this year. The club members also support Children's Village in Beijing, a home for 115 children (whose parents are in prison), members work with a school for autistic children, and help to refurbish schools in Tibet. In addition, they are working to establish Rotary International Sponsored Service Clubs: Rotaract (serving men and women ages 18 to 30) and Interact (serving youth ages 12 to 18) in Beijing to provide the community easy access to a variety of ongoing volunteer opportunities. The 52 members come from 12 countries, including Chinese from Hong Kong and other countries. Most members are CEOs or senior managers from a variety of industries including, airline, hotel, banking, consulting, public relations, law, energy, information technology, pharmaceuticals, and automobile manufacturing.

Representative of the United States to the Office of the UN at Geneva, Ambassador Betty E. King

Ambassador Betty E. King served as the United States Representative to the Economic and Social Council of the United Nations under Presidents Bill Clinton and George W. Bush. In that capacity, she worked on human rights, development, children, aging, and population issues. She was the principal US negotiator on the Millennium Development Goals.

Ambassador King has an extensive background in philanthropy having served as Vice President of the Annie E. Casey Foundation, an organization dedicated to improving the lives of disadvantaged children. She served as the Senior Advisor to the CEO of the California Endowment where she worked to improve health services and systems, and as an advisor to Atlantic Philanthropies on their programs for children and youth.

In the public sector, Ambassador King has served as the Deputy Commissioner for Mental Health Services in the District of Columbia, as the Director of the Department on Aging in Arkansas, and as an Assistant Professor at the University of Arkansas. She currently serves on the boards of Refugees International, The United Nations Association of the United States, Phoenix House, and on the Advisory Board of the Annenberg School of Public Diplomacy.

Ambassador King earned a bachelor of arts degree at the University of Windsor, Ontario, Canada, a master's degree at the State University of New York at Stony Brook, was a National Humanities Fellow at Harvard University, and a Public Policy Fellow at the University of California, Los Angeles.

Permanent Observer of Palestine to the UN, H.E. Mr. Riyad Mansour

His Excellency, Mr. Riyad Mansour stressed the importance of the two-state solution on the basis of the pre-1967 borders and the longstanding parameters enshrined in the relevant United Nations Resolutions, Madrid Principles, Arab Peace Initiative, and the Quartet Roadmap.

In April 2014, President Mahmoud Abbas signed fifteen instruments of accession to multilateral treaties, affirming the State of Palestine's acceptance of the principles therein, readiness to uphold legal obligations, and commitment to promoting the rights of the Palestinian people in accordance with the law. Among those are the core treaties of international humanitarian law: the four Geneva Conventions, Additional Protocol 1 and the 1907 Hague Convention, the core human rights treaties including among others, the International Covenants on Civil and Political Rights and also on Economic, Social, and Cultural Rights, Convention on the Rights of the Child, Convention on the Elimination of All Forms of Discrimination against Women, Convention on the Rights of Persons with Disabilities, and the International Convention on the Suppression and Punishment of the Crime of Apartheid.

The Deputy Ambassador of the Russian Federation, H.E. Mr. Konstantin Dolgov

The Deputy Ambassador of the Russian Federation, H.E. Mr. Konstantin Dolgov, was the guest speaker at our International Breakfast Meeting. He presented an enlightening assessment of several of the notable issues facing today's United Nations. He stated that since the end of the Cold War, the UN has successfully maintained stability in many areas of the world due to its peacekeeping operations. In his view, the UN is uniquely suited to remain as the international community's principal forum for peacekeeping and conflict resolution because of its unmatched universality, legitimacy, and organizational structure.

Currently there are approximately 70,000 UN personnel, serving in 17 peacekeeping operations. He noted that the 18th operation would commence within a few weeks once the UN begins assistance in the Sudan.

The UN is also responsible to coordinate humanitarian assistance, social rehabilitation, and institution building in many of these areas of conflict. The Russian Federation currently provides several hundred peacekeepers in several areas of conflict under the UN banner and expects to expand its contribution.

The Ambassador also made it apparent that the War on Terrorism, nuclear proliferation by nongovernmental groups, as well as economic underdevelopment are all vital concerns in which the UN will be effective.

He expounded that the UN in not capable of solving all global issues but that its most useful function is to act as "the" international hub to offer an organizational umbrella and legal framework for the coalition of the willing. Above all, the UN is the only international forum that can authorize the use of military force on behalf of the international community.

He also spoke about Security Council reform stressing that, contrary to popular opinion, the UN is not a supranational organization. Rather, it is an intergovernmental organization that can only achieve what the Member States require it to accomplish. The UN's efficacy is entirely in the hands of the Member States.

He congratulated Rotarians because in many ways the Rotarian voluntary mission typifies the best example of human instinct in action. Rotary International is:

- Community based and community driven,
- Democratically sustained,
- Effectively run,
- Generous in spirit and reach,
- Global in membership and vision.

Mr. Francis Dubois, Frequent Guest and Moderator

The guest speaker at the February, 2009 International Breakfast Meeting was Mr. Francis Dubois. Born in Alsace, France, Mr. DuBois had a distinguished career within the United Nations. He was first stationed in Uganda, then in New York City before being assigned to the Palestinian Territories where he served as Deputy Coordinator of the Secretary-General. Mr. Dubois was then posted to Iraq as the Head of the UN Office (with the rank of Ambassador), and subsequently Algeria and

Tunisia in the same capacity. Mr. Dubois is an active member of several interreligious nongovernmental organizations and serves on numerous boards. He lives in New York City. The meeting was moderated by Wall Street Rotarian, Sheila Washington.

UN Peacekeeping Operations, Major General Randhir Kumar Mehta

Major General Randhir Kumar Mehta of India is the Military Advisor in the Department of Peacekeeping Operations in 2005. With a distinguished career in the Indian Army holding numerous national command and staff positions and serving as a Sector Commander with UNAMSIL (United Nations Mission in Sierra Leone) from May 2000 to February 2001.The General has also been a member of India's delegation in various peace talks. He is a graduate of the National Defense Services Staff College, the Higher Command Course of the National Defense College, and holds Masters of Sciences and Philosophy Degrees. Major General Mehta has been honored by the President of India with the "Yudh Seva Medal" for gallantry in operations in Sierra Leone and the "Vishisht Seva Medal" for Distinguished Services of a High Order.

Certain factors are critical for the success of any UN peacekeeping operation:

- The international community must diagnose the problem correctly before prescribing peacekeeping as the treatment
- There must be a "peace to keep"; all key parties to the conflict must consent to stop fighting, accept the UN role in helping them resolve their dispute, and agree to the deployment of a UN Peacekeeping Mission.
- Members of the Security Council must agree on a clear and achievable mandate.
- Deployment must proceed quickly.

United Nations peace operations entail four principal activities:

- Conflict prevention—addresses the structural sources of conflict
- Peacemaking—conflict in progress

- Peacekeeping—maintains an existing peace
- Peacebuilding—rebuilds government and democratic infrastructure to create a solid foundation for peace.

Currently, there are approximately 70,000 “blue helmets”: 34% from Asia, 28% from Africa, the rest from South America and Middle East.

There are seventeen Missions worldwide located in Sudan, Burundi, Côte d’Ivoire, Liberia, Congo, Ethiopia, Haiti, Timor-Leste, India /Pakistan Border, Cyprus, Georgia, Kosovo, Golan Heights, Lebanon, and Jerusalem.

Croatian Ambassador Mladineo Outlines Useful Model for Small-State Nationalism

Ambassador Ms. Mirjana Mladineo earned advanced degrees in English and Russian Languages and Culture, from the University of Zagreb. Before her position at the UN, she was Head of the Croatian Mission to the EU Ministry for European Integration; National Coordinator for the Central European Initiative; Minister Counselor at the UN in New York from 1992 to 1997; Department Head of the Republic Administration for Scientific and Technical International Cooperation; and Counselor for the Republic Committee for Education, Culture, Technical Culture, and Sports.

Ambassador Mladineo informed the guests that she was a charter member of a Rotary Club in Croatia, she had to resign due to professional relocation, but hopes to someday to rejoin.

When she was first assigned to the UN as a Counselor in 1992, her country was still in a state of crisis. Croatia had just ended a twelve-year war and had just become a sovereign state. However, since that time, she noted that Croatia has made significant progress and has been a useful model for a number of countries transforming into a stable, market economy, and parliamentary democracy after emerging from war.

She emphasized that during the war, the UN and the International community were very effective in providing international peacekeeping forces that were very much engaged in former Yugoslavia. In 1995, after the UN withdrawal, we were able to develop our own resources and develop our own country. “If it were not for UN assistance, Croatia would not be where it is today.” This was especially true when there were 800,000 refugees or displaced persons due to the conflict.

She also noted that Croatia condemns all war crimes, is committed to bringing war criminals to justice, and supports the International Criminal Tribunal of the former Yugoslavia.

Currently, the Ambassador noted that European Union membership is essential to her country's overall economic development initiated at the Zagreb Summit in November, 2000. Internal reforms to facilitate market-based economic development, reorganization of state administration, and full implementation of all European democratic standards is required before Croatia will be granted membership to the EU. These reforms also include the rule of law, guarantee of civil and religious freedoms, and complete equality for all our citizens. Achieving these reforms has transformed our country from a command-based economy to an open, demand-based market economy. Fortunately, a high percentage of our citizens support the transformation, she noted.

Our tourist trade is the most promising industry of Croatia with our beautiful shoreline and Croatia's 1400 islands.

It is the priority of Croatia to build its international and security position based on NATO (North Atlantic Treaty Organization) membership. Actively preparing to join NATO, Croatia is ready to fulfill obligations for membership.

In summary, The Ambassador noted that joining the European Union and transforming economic integration, solving open issues remaining after the breakup of the former Yugoslavia, establishing good neighbor relations and cooperation with neighboring countries based on principles of equality and reciprocity are the main issues facing her country now.

UNICEF Goodwill Ambassador and Actress, Mia Farrow

Award winning film actress, Mia Farrow personally thanked New York City area and Bermuda Rotarians for the nearly complete eradication of polio from the planet. She spoke at the Rotary District 7230 Annual Conference held in Tarrytown, New York on April 28, 2006.

Ms. Farrow was appointed UNICEF (United Nations International Children's Fund) Goodwill Ambassador in 2000. Since then, she has visited Nigeria and many other developing countries to participate in polio immunization campaigns on behalf of the United Nations in partnership with Rotary International. Ms. Farrow joined the ranks of thousands of health professionals and volunteers as they have nearly immunized every child under the age of five.

Ms. Farrow fell victim to polio when she was nine years old while growing up in affluent Beverly Hills, California. She remembers those days well, and it changed her outlook on life. In addition, her adoptive son, Thaddeus, who was born in India, also contracted polio and is wheelchair dependent. Ms. Farrow and her family subsequently live the devastating effects of polio every day. She told Rotarians that her son's legs are atrophied and he needs to drag himself along the floor by his arms when he is not in a wheelchair. Ms. Farrow told Rotarians, "In this great country of ours we make a lot of accommodations, but in the developing world everyday life for polio victims is much more difficult. But thanks to the efforts of Rotary, 1.4 million children have been spared from this disease."

In her friendly and personable manner, the actress presented District Governor and Past President of the Rotary Club of New York, Helen Reisler, with a plaque thanking all Rotarians for the quest to eradicate polio. In return, Governor Reisler presented the Goodwill Ambassador with a Paul Harris Fellowship and Ms. Farrow graciously accepted it on behalf of the 1.4 million children Rotary's program has saved. She asked that Rotarians invite her back once the PolioPlus Program was completed and the world was certified polio-free.

Ambassador of Iraq Visit to Thank Gift of Life, H.E. Samir Shakir Mahmood Sumaida'ie

Ambassador Samir Shakir Mahmood Sumaida'ie visited the Rotary Club of New York's monthly International Breakfast Meeting at the United Nations to thank Rotarians for arranging and financing high-risk heart surgery at a New York hospital for six Iraqi children. Rotary's Gift of Life has arranged this surgical procedure for more than 9,000 children over the last twenty years, but these are the first children from Iraq. The children, all boys, range in age from six years old to fourteen years old, were accompanied by their fathers, and have been in New York for about two weeks. They have all fully recovered, and are now expected to live a long and healthy life.

The Ambassador emphasized that this Rotary service project was indeed a Gift of Life, but it was also a "Gift of Goodwill." Their families and friends will remember the generosity and humanity of Americans for years to come.

He outlined another recent situation of a young mother who needed extensive eye reconstruction from a terrorist-inflicted injury. A prominent Iraqi surgeon, practicing in New York, donated the surgery and hospital costs, and the Ambassador arranged for housing and transportation.

Ambassador Sumaida'ie noted that obviously, there is a great need for this type of humanitarian work, and there are many cases that need attention. These acts of humanity are also important because they resonate in people's memories. People witness, firsthand, the humanity of Americans, as well as all nationalities that are part of the Rotary Club of New York. "We must all feel we are one human family, and this is where hope for the future lies," he concluded.

Permanent Representative of Belgium, H.E. Ms. Bénédicte Frankinet

Before her appointment as Permanent Representative of Belgium to the United Nations, H.E. Ms. Bénédicte Frankinet served as Ambassador to Israel since 2008 after previously serving as Director for the United Nations at the Ministry of Foreign Affairs in Brussels since 2003. From 1999 to 2003, Ms. Frankinet was Ambassador to Zimbabwe, accredited also to Mozambique, Malawi, and Zambia. Between 1994 and 1999, she served as Counsellor, then Deputy Head of the Mission at her country's embassy in Paris. In 1992, Ms. Frankinet was an Advisor in the private office of the Minister for Foreign Affairs, and from 1988 to 1992, she was First Secretary at Belgium's Permanent Representation to the European Communities in Brussels.

She served a previous appointment between 1983 and 1988, at the New York Permanent Mission as First Secretary, and was an attaché in Brasilia from 1979 to 1983. Ms. Frankinet holds degrees in political science, social science, and journalism from the Free University of Brussels.

Like RI (Rotary International), Belgium is an important donor to the development programs of the UN System. In 2005 Belgian contributions amounted to 184 million euro, or 12% of its total official development assistance. Belgium plays an active role in the executive boards of UNDP

(United Nations Development Programme), UNICEF (United Nations Children's Fund), UNFPA (United Nations Population Fund), UNIFEM (United Nations Development Fund for Women), and UNCDF (United Nations Capital Development Fund), and in consultations between these funds and programs and the major donor countries.

In its relationship with the funds and programs, Belgium strongly emphasizes the implementation of the Millennium Development Goals and the 2005 Paris Declaration on Aid Effectiveness.

When funding programs of UNDP, UNICEF, UNFPA, UNIFEM, and UNCDF, Belgium tries to concentrate on a limited number of themes it feels are essential for development such as: support to subsidiary administration and local development, and good governance—in particular the strengthening of parliaments and support of election processes. On March 14-15, 2007, Belgium will host an "International Conference on Good Governance" in Brussels focusing on the fight against the abuse of children and women, particularly in post-conflict zones.

Permanent Representative of Israel, Ambassador Daniel Carmon

Permanent Representative of Israel, Ambassador Daniel Carmon spoke about UN Reform and Israel. Ambassador Carmon was born in Tel Aviv and attended schools in Jerusalem and Paris, and served as a Paratrooper in the Israeli Defense Force. He was awarded a BA in International Affairs from Hebrew University in 1973. He started his career with the Ministry of Foreign Affairs and served in Washington and Argentina, 1996-2000 as Department of Public Affairs Director and now Deputy Permanent Representative to the United Nations for Israel. He noted that he has had many contacts with Rotary over the years.

There was high hope when the State of Israel was established after World War II and entered the newly established UN. Membership in the UN promised democracy, equal representation, and equality of rights for all members. However, once the organization entered adolescence, the UN mechanism was being misused, and Israel was being treated differently than other Member States. He pointed out that "inside politics" allowed Israel to be denied its basic rights as a member of the organization.

He detailed some of the shortfalls of the current model. For example, the UN Charter gives every member the right to membership in the Security Council; membership is decided according to geographic distribution, and council members are selected from the five geographical groupings.

Geographically, Israel should belong to the Asian group. However, because of political differences with its neighbors, Israel was not accepted into the Asian Group. Therefore, it had to be given indefinite, temporary, membership in the WEOG (Western Europe and Others Group). As a result, for many years Israel could not be considered a candidate or nominated for any position.

He also pointed out the long list of UN resolutions concerning Israel every year. The current system allows voting-blocks to pass or reject any resolution, no matter how one-sided. He noted that there is no connection between the resolutions and diplomatic advances made. Every year the same nineteen or so one-sided resolutions are introduced.

He also noted that Emergency Special Sessions were primarily held on Israeli issues. It was also pointed out that over 25% of the condemnations issued by the Commission on Human Rights referred to Israel.

The Ambassador said that he is only talking about the Middle East. He is sure that the same inside politics is going on in the other regions. For example, in such recent genocides such as Rwanda, the Balkans, and the current situation in Sudan, the UN paralyzed itself and was unable to take any action.

There are, however, hopeful and symbolic events taking place. Mr. Dan Gillerman, the Permanent Representative of Israel to the UN was elected as the Vice President of the 60th UN General Assembly. The last Israeli elected to this post was Abba Eban in 1952. While Ambassador Gillerman is only one of twenty-one vice presidents, it was considered an historic and significant event in Israel. In addition, Israel is being considered for a position on the Security Council in 2018. Again, he emphasized, it is symbolic that we have even been considered. Just a few years back, Israel would not have been able to even be proposed as a candidate. The Ambassador credits these advances with the help of its many friends in the UN such as many countries in Europe, the United States, Canada, and Australia.

Ambassador Carmon is very interested in reading the upcoming recommendations of the United States Congressional Committee on UN reform. Hopefully its recommendations will make the UN more effective in providing equal rights and representation to all its members.

Mr. Ban Ki-moon, Secretary-General of the United Nations

Mr. Ban Ki-moon, was scheduled to address the conference but had to unexpectedly travel to Nairobi, Kenya for the African Union Regional Summit on the conflict situation in the eastern Democratic Republic of the Congo.

His welcoming letter, which follows, was read by Mr. Kim Won-soo who has been the Deputy Chef de Cabinet since January 2007 and Assistant to the Secretary-General. Prior to that he served as Ambassador of the Republic of Korea as head of the Transition Team for the eighth Secretary-General of the United Nations.

> *Dear Rotary International President Lee and Rotarians:*
>
> *It is a great pleasure to welcome you all to the United Nations. It is always a pleasure to host Rotary International. We share your commitment to securing global public goods, and we value the energy you bring to global challenges. Ours is a good, long-standing partnership. Today we need your hard work more than ever.*
>
> *Earlier this year, I started speaking about what I describe as "a people crisis." Soaring prices for food and fuel, accelerating climate change, and stalled development for the world's poorest people, are some thoughts I was eager to raise. Today, we see that if anything, it was an understatement. The global financial crisis has brought an additional shock compounding all the others. Although it may have receded from the headlines, the food crisis is still very much with us. Food and fertilizer prices are two times as high as they were one year ago. Climate change is worse with every passing day and some ask how we can take steps to prevent climate change in the middle of this financial crisis. But given the situation, we can*

create 'green jobs' and spur investment. I ask, how we can offer not to.

And progress toward the Millennium Development Goals has been uneven; many countries are falling behind especially in Sub-Saharan Africa. We hear about how our problems on Wall Street affects people on Main Street. We also need to think about people around the world even with no streets at all. A series of upcoming meetings provide an opportunity to get back on track. These include the G-20 gathering in Washington, the Finance for Development Conference later this month in Doha, and climate negotiations early next month in Poznań, Poland. We must make the most of these occasions.

Partnerships will be crucial as we move ahead. The United Nations attaches great importance to close ties with Rotary International, and it is grateful to the contributions you have made to global health, education, and poverty eradication efforts. We also look forward to working with the administration of the new President Elect Obama, who has spoken often of the importance of diplomacy, international cooperation, and especially strong United Nations. Together we must deliver results for a safer, healthier, and a more prosperous world. It is encouraging to know that the United Nations will continue to be able to count on Rotary International to do its part. Please accept my best wishes for a memorable day at the United Nations. I thank you.

Mr. Ban Ki-moon,
Secretary-General of the United Nations

Pope Benedict XVI

Upon arriving at the United Nations, Pope Benedict XVI was welcomed by the UN Secretary-General, Mr. Ban Ki-moon, and the President of the General Assembly, H.E. Dr. Srgjan Kerim. Before addressing the General Assembly, Pope Benedict met privately with the Secretary-General.

He noted that the founding principles of the United Nations—

the desire for peace, a sense of justice, respect for the dignity of the human person, and cooperation and humanitarian assistance—are just aspirations of the human spirit. The Holy See shares an interest in these principles.

Questions of security, development, reducing inequality, and care of the environment require collective action in good faith for the common good. While scientific and technological advances can be of great help, some can rob the human person and the family of their identity. He called on the international community to act with juridical means when needed to safeguard human rights.

The Holy Father spoke of the critical importance of protecting human rights, noting the sixtieth anniversary of the Universal Declaration of Human Rights. Promoting human rights is the most effective strategy for reducing inequality and increasing security. Human rights are not simply a matter of law, but of justice, based in the natural law written on the human heart.

Once again, the Holy Father spoke of the importance of dialogue between religions as a way of building consensus in service of the common good. He emphasized the importance of freedom of religion in its public as well as its private dimension.

Pope Benedict said that the Catholic Church wishes to offer her proper contribution to international relations, making available her centuries of experience. He concluded his address by greeting the Assembly in all the official languages of the United Nations, wishing them peace and prosperity with God's help.

The Assembly responded to his address with a standing ovation.

From their website:
https://usccb.wordpress.com/2008/04/18/pope-benedict-xvi-addresses-the-united-nations-general-assembly/

Pope Benedict XVI was the third Pope to address the United Nations following Pope Paul VI and Pope John Paul II. (Pope John Paul II addressed the United Nations twice, in 1979 and in 1995.)

German Mission, Ms. Victoria Zimmermann Von Siefart, Minister Plenipotentiary and Head of the Economic Department

Ms. Victoria Zimmermann Von Siefart has worked with the German Foreign Service since 1985 and has an impressive background of heading Foreign Service Departments in London, Philippines, Switzerland, and New York. Ms. Zimmermann Von Siefart was born in Bombay, India, was educated in the Netherlands and Germany, and studied in Paris, Freiburg in Breisgau, and Bonn.

According to the 2008 Trends in the *Sustainable Development Report* published by the Department of Economic and Social Affairs, efforts to reduce poverty and improve food security in developing countries are hampered by declining support for strong agricultural growth, long considered a hallmark of successful poverty reduction strategies.

The Report highlights recent trends in agriculture, rural development, land, desertification and drought—five of the six themes being considered by the Commission on Sustainable Development at its 16th and 17th sessions (2008-2009).

The Report reveals that strong agricultural growth is four times more effective than growth in other sectors in benefiting the poorest half of the population. However, while many developing countries have posted gains in agricultural production, distribution and exports, people living in areas of high inequality and in isolation from the broader economy typically benefit little from them.

UN Under-Secretary-General, John Holmes

The United Nations Secretary-General established a Task Force on the Global Food Security Crisis under his chairmanship composed of leaders of United Nations specialized agencies, funds and programs, Bretton Woods Institutions, and relevant parts of the UN Secretariat. The primary aim of the Task Force is to promote a unified response to the global food price challenge, which includes facilitating the creation of a prioritized plan of action and coordinating its implementation. The Secretary-General appointed UN Under-Secretary-General John Holmes as Task Force Coordinator and Assistant Secretary-General David Nabarro as Deputy Coordinator.

"Singapore's Ambassador to the United Nations, H.E. Vanu Gopala Menon" By Sheila Washington, *(Visiting Rotarian from San Diego, California)*

It was Wednesday, April 19th, and at 8:30 a.m. the Rotary Club, NY was in session on the top floor of the German Mission. It was a beautiful spring morning for a room full of members, guests, and the keynote speaker, Ambassador Vanu Gopala Menon. The Ambassador is Singapore's Permanent Representative to the United Nations in New York, and concurrently Singapore's High Commissioner to Canada.

After an excellent breakfast, opening remarks, and announcements, Coordinator and Moderator Joe Klee of the International Division of the NY Rotary introduced Ambassador Menon. Born in Singapore, September 8, 1960, Ambassador Menon joined the Ministry of Foreign Affairs in June 1985. He served in many leadership positions, including Singapore's Chief Negotiator for the Singapore-Australia Free Trade Agreement and Chairman of the World Trade Organization's Council for TRIPS (Trade Related Intellectual Property Rights) from 2003-2004. He presented his credentials to the United Nations in September 2004.

In his overview, the Ambassador's comments reminded us that the UN has evolved from an institution founded to prevent war into an umbrella organization whose work today revolves around a seemingly ambitious and open-ended agenda. Its scope of work includes, but is not limited to: human rights, economic development, world health, child welfare, women's rights, international justice, trade, and intellectual property, among other tasks. The UN has been praised for helping eliminate apartheid in South Africa, coordinating the mammoth relief effort for the 2004 tsunami in Southeast Asia and setting benchmarks for combating global poverty, hunger, and disease as part of its Millennium Development Goals. It is not usual for the UN to be the first responder coordinating efforts in times of global crisis.

However, its long list of accomplishments is usually trumped by a short list of hot-button items that create and rule its image. This includes the stronger image of the Oil-for-Food Programme in Iraq amidst allegation of corruption, peacekeepers accused of various crimes, and its seemingly ineffective human-rights commission.

The UN began with about 50 states. In its 60th year, there are 191 Member States.

Supporters and critics alike agree that the United Nations needs an overhaul, both physically and institutionally. In addition, its governance and management are under attack from many directions.

The Ambassador highlighted issues for the reform process:

- *Building a Peacekeeping Force that stands on its own:* In most countries, the UN has the Good Housekeeping Seal of Approval and has proved itself effective in peacekeeping efforts. Historically, small and medium-sized countries are more likely to act at the request of the UN than from an individual country. However, there is no standing UN peacekeeping force for timely assignment.
- *Restructuring of the Discredited Human Rights Commission:* It currently takes a two-thirds vote to remove a Member State from the Commission. A change to simple majority is one of the proposals under consideration.
- *Investing In Development:* Both developed and developing countries have a stake in development as globalization races on it present new and fast-moving challenges to the Member States. In a final report to the UN in 2005, an action plan was outlined to achieve the goal to cut world poverty by half in a decade. Will the Member States seize the opportunity to take action?
- *Adapting True Management Reform:* Secretary-General Annan announced in March a bottom-up look at how the Secretariat should be managed. The plan includes taking certain functions out of New York and implementing rigorous monitoring for more transparency of processes and procedures.
- *Image Building:* Recalling that the United States took the lead in the creation of the UN, there is currently a substantial and vocal hostility to the UN being in the United States. How can the UN promote the UN in the United States?

Looking Ahead

The General Assembly remains a place for discussion and achieving consensus on these and other issues. The awesome veto power of the Security Council membership of five, seemed to be lessened since the end of the Cold War because there is a general consensus that the world is interconnected, and for all practical purposes, has no borders. The biggest challenge ahead for these two main bodies is the selection of the next Secretary-General by the end of 2006. The outcome of that process will be most telling for the UN's future.

Creating a more effective format for explaining the UN and a common understanding of its goals for the general public's consumption is under consideration. For instance, directing some criticism directly at the Member State may be more appropriate. If a problem were to go to the Security Council and one of its members blocked meaningful action, is it fair to consider that action a failure of the UN, or for the record, is it the result of a UN State that prevented the UN from doing its job?

In summary, the Ambassador gave Rotarians a sensitive and comprehensive picture of the UN today. He expressed deeply the commitment of his country to a vital UN that can meet its challenges effectively. It was also gratifying to learn of the dedicated work of his delegation over the years to effect meaningful change that is consistent with the global challenges.

On the face of it, it seems that since its 60th anniversary summit, the UN is taking steps to make the adjustment needed for a comprehensive overhaul of its operating structure and management.

And so it was on a beautiful spring morning in April. As we headed off in different directions, there was a better understanding, and just maybe, the knowledge that momentum for reform can be sustained. At the UN today, the glass is half full.

The hope for a better way of life for most people on this planet is still alive.

THE UNITED NATIONS ADMINISTRATORS

The ICSC (International Civil Service Commission) of the United Nations General Assembly is charged with the regulation and coordination of the conditions of service for the United Nations common system staff. The Secretary-General of the United Nations heads the administrative arm of day-to-day work of the UN as mandated by the General Assembly and the organization's other principal organs. However, some major Director-Generals are elected by their respective organizations. For example, the Director of the World Health Organization is elected by the General Conference of the WHO every four years, as is the Director-General of the ENESCO. Most of the other directors are appointed by the Secretary-General in cooperation with the department managers.

Clean Water: the World's Most Precious Resource

UNICEF reports that 30% of childhood diseases in developing regions are attributable to contaminated water. Therefore, for our 100th anniversary, Rotarians have formulated a major program that is geared toward developing clean water resources around the world.

Our emphasis is concentrated on the following:

- Promote conservation of water resources
- Assist communities in cleaning up lakes, rivers, streams, and other water resources

- Provide water wells, and other sources of water, to low-income communities
- Demonstrate effective partnerships with local organizations, Ministries of Health, and other organizations that provide water resource management
- Provide assistance to farmers regarding water use

We will also address the UN program known as WASH (the Water, Sanitation, and Hygiene) program. On November 6, 2004, we will have United Nation's Day for Rotary. Our organization's president will be there as well as past presidents and our board of directors. The main topics for discussion will be water and sanitation. The other areas of discussion at UN Day will be Polio and HIV/AIDS. We will continue our work on guinea worm, measles, and especially dysentery, which is caused by dirty water and sanitation. We now have a letter exchange with UNESCO (United Nations Educational, Scientific and Cultural Organization) that was signed in December, 2003 to promote joint projects.

Regarding the PolioPlus Program, we hope to complete this program by the end of this year. We are now down to about 300 cases worldwide. These cases are in West Africa, Nigeria, and India. It should be pointed out that India is an incredible story: Excluding two years ago, there was a sudden outbreak of about 1000 cases in India. Right now, the count is down to less than 100 cases. Now we will demonstrate the same efforts to provide safe drinking water.

A Canadian national, Ms. Anne Kerr is the Chief of Program Coordination, Major Groups and Partnerships Branch, Division for Sustainable Development at the DESA (United Nations Department of Economic and Social Affairs). She earned a Bachelor's Degree in Geography from the University of British Columbia, Vancouver and a Master's Degree in Regional Planning and Resource Development from the University of Waterloo in Ontario.

Anne joined the United Nations in November 2001 as Chief, National Information, Strategies and Institutions Branch, DSD (Division of Sustainable Development) Secretariat, and was involved in tracking the substantive sessions of the preparatory meeting for the WSSD (World Summit on Sustainable Development) as well as the

World Summit on Sustainable Development itself, held in Johannesburg, South Africa in 2002.

For over 25 years, Ms. Kerr worked with the Canadian government, managed Canada's National Environmental Indicators Program from 1990 to 2001, and represented Canada internationally in the field. Please welcome Ms. Anne Kerr.

Anne Kerr began her address. First of all, I would like to thank the Rotary Club of New York for inviting me to this morning's meeting. I am indeed honored to be here during your organization's 100th year. I also bring greetings from Ms. Joanne DiSano, Director of the Division for Sustainable Development.

I was asked to lead a discussion related to sustainable development and poverty eradication in least developed countries. I am going to focus my remarks on a review of the progress toward three key targets related to poverty eradication that are the themes for the 12th session of the CSD (Commission on Sustainable Development) taking place in April this year, while also making references to the LDCs (Least Developed Countries).

First let me start with a quote from the Johannesburg Declaration on Sustainable Development about the challenges we face. "We recognize that poverty eradication, changing consumption and production patterns, and protecting and managing the natural resource base for economic and social development are overarching objectives of, and essential requirements for, sustained development."

Eradicating poverty has been called the greatest global challenge facing the world today, and for the 600 million people living in the 50 least developed countries, the special support and initiatives for poverty eradication called for in the Brussels Program of Action for LDCs cannot come too soon.

The main focus of the United Nations CSD (Commission on Sustainable Development) is the implementation of the JPOI (Johannesburg Plan of Implementation)—a plan that covers all aspects of the Brussels Program of Action.

At its 11th session in 2003, CSD set out a program of work up to the year 2017 to make progress towards the implementation of targets, commitments, and goals made in Agenda 21 and the JPOI—the latter agreed to the WSSD in Johannesburg in 2002. The work program comprises two-year action-oriented implementation cycles—a review year and a policy year. The review year is to evaluate the progress, obstacles, constraints, successes, and lessons learned. The policy year is to determine further actions required to accelerate and enhance implementation and overcome obstacles.

The upcoming 12th session of the Commission on Sustainable Development will review sustainable development commitments in the area of water, sanitation, and human settlements.

Drawing from the Secretary-General's reports prepared for CSD-12 just released, which review progress in meeting goals, targets, and commitments of Agenda 21, the Program for Further Implementation of Agenda 21, and the Johannesburg Plan of Implementation, I am going to focus on three targets which relate particularly to LDCs.

First, to halve by the year 2015, the proportion of people who are unable to reach or to afford safe drinking water; second, to halve by the year 2015, the proportion of people who do not have access to basic sanitation. The third target is to achieve by the year 2020 a significant improvement in the lives of at least 100 million slum dwellers.

Let me start with the last one, first. Slums are characterized by substandard housing, overcrowding, insecure tenure, and lack of basic services such as safe water, improved sanitation, transportation, and electricity. They exist in run-down inner city neighborhoods, urban fringe squatter areas, or shanty towns.

According to UN Habitat, slum populations make up 6% of urban populations in developed countries, 43% of the population in the developing countries, and a whopping 78% of the population in least developing countries. If the current trend continues, the number of slum dwellers worldwide is projected to rise from the current 924 million to about 2 billion over the next 30 years. Basic services and infrastructure must be provided if the crushing impact of poverty, social exclusion, and unhealthy living conditions in slums are to be mitigated. It should be pointed out that developed countries spend on average, 32 times more per person on infrastructure and urban services than cities in LDCs.

The second target is access to safe drinking water. I know that this is an area of great concern to Rotarians. Contaminated drinking water is a major source of illness and death in developing countries. During the 1990s, the number of people with access to improved drinking water supply increased from 70% of the global population to 82% in 2000. This represents significant progress but is well below the rate required to meet the 2015 target. The greatest gains were in South Asia, which is on track to meet the target. However, sub-Saharan Africa and Oceania have the lowest access rates—58% and 48% respectively. The challenge in sub-Saharan Africa is more complex due to large displaced and refugee populations, countries in conflict or reconstruction, and HIV/AIDS pandemics.

There are wide disparities in access for safe drinking water between urban and rural populations. In the least developed countries, 38% of the population is without access to improved drinking water. This is segmented—18% in urban areas and 45% in rural areas. Based on current urban and rural access rates and using projected population figures, an additional 358 million people in LDCs will need access to improved drinking water to meet the 2015 target.

So, what needs to be done? In terms of slums, proactive shelter provision policies and programs that seek to avert further slum growth and encourage expansion of low-cost housing stock and associated infrastructure need to be implemented locally. Slum upgrading and integration, rather that eradication of slums and relocation of slum dwellers, will be more effective since it must be noted that past eradication of slums has destroyed large stocks of affordable housing and simply displaced slum dwellers from one informal settlement to another.

Access to credit markets and job creations programs will also be helpful.

Regarding safe drinking water: contaminated water sources, inadequate maintenance of pumps and distribution systems and leakage of water from pipes are the main problems that need to be overcome. Due to the increasing financial and environmental costs of developing new sources of water, it is generally more cost-effective to increase the "effective" water supply by reducing leakage and water losses. Improved sanitation is essential to increasing the availability of safe drinking water and improving living conditions in human settlements. However, very few countries have incorporated sanitation programs explicitly in their national development and poverty reduction strategies.

The recent Secretary-General's report for CSD-12 reviewed progress in providing access to improved sanitation in dispersed rural settlements, medium-density communities and high-density urban communities. Among other things, education and awareness-raising programs have to build demand for sanitation technologies appropriate to the conditions. Many NGOs and community organizations have mobilized substantial resources for sanitation for both facilities and awareness-raising. Rotary International is an example of an organization with tremendous ability to mobilize resources in this area.

I would like to conclude with another quote from the Johannesburg Declaration on Sustainable Development regarding our commitment to sustainable development: "We recognize the reality that a global society has the means, and is endowed with, the resources to address the challenges of poverty, eradication, and sustainable development confronting all humanity. Together, we will take extra steps to ensure that these available resources are used to the benefit of humanity."

We salute Rotary International's 100 years of efforts on taking those extra steps to confront the challenge. And I would recommend Rotarians to log on to our website at *http://www.un.org/esa/sustdev/* and click on to the "Partnership" section. There you will find a database of more than 260 "Partnership Initiatives" that your respective clubs may find useful. In addition, the upcoming "Partnership Fair" at CSD-12 will offer a number of booths and videos that will help identify potential projects.

WHO (World Health Organization) Fight Against Polio, Andrey V. Pirogov

Mr. Andrey V. Pirogov, Assistant Executive Director of the WHO Office at the UN was the guest speaker at the February 25, 2008 International Breakfast Meeting.

He joined WHO in 2006 as Executive Director of the WHO Office at the United Nations in New York. Prior to that, he was Deputy Permanent Representative of Russia in Geneva, and in this capacity served as the principal counterpart to WHO and other multilateral health institutions. He has been involved in UN affairs for more than 20 years. Mr. Pirogov graduated from the Moscow Institute of International Relations in 1977. He joined the diplomatic service of his country the same year and has since held a wide range of diplomatic posts in the

Foreign Ministry of the USSR and Russia.

Mr. Pirogov's professional appointments include positions with the USSR Embassy to Cameroon, the Russian Mission to the European Communities in Brussels, and participation in numerous international conferences. During his diplomatic career, Mr. Pirogov gained wide experience with the organizations of the UN System and in such areas as European security, relations between Russia and the EU, disarmament, international security, and the external economic relations of Russia.

The WHO (World Health Organization) is the directing and coordinating authority for health within the United Nations System. It is responsible for providing leadership on global health matters, shaping the health research agenda, setting norms and standards, articulating evidence-based policy options, providing technical support to countries, and monitoring and assessing health trends. The organization's goals include:

- Promoting development
- Fostering health security
- Strengthening health systems
- Harnessing research, information, and evidence
- Enhancing partnerships

Mr. Pirogov as does the WHO recognized Rotary International's PolioPlus Program established in 1985. Rotary was the first to have the vision of a polio-free world, and continues to play a crucial role in global efforts to eradicate polio. More than one million Rotary members have volunteered their time and personal resources to protect more than 2 billion children in 122 countries from polio.

Rotary provides urgently needed funds—to date, the organization has contributed more than US $500 million, and raised an additional US $119 million in 2003. In addition, Rotary's Polio Eradication Advocacy Task Force has played a major role in decisions by donor governments to contribute more than US $1.5 billion to the effort. That amount, combined with direct funds from Rotary, is more than half the money needed for the entire global polio eradication program. Rotary members also provide valuable field support during National Immunization Days through social mobilization and by administering the oral polio vaccine to children.

Mr. Carlos G. Ruiz Massieu, Representative of the Mission of Mexico to the United Nations

Mr. Ruiz Massieu is the Chairman of the United Nations Advisory Committee on Administrative and Budgetary Questions which has complete oversight of all UN activities, including its political missions and peacekeeping operations worldwide. He is the first Latin American to hold this position in the history of the United Nations.

Mexican citizen Carlos Ruiz Massieu Aguirre was appointed chairman of the UN's Advisory Committee on ACABQ (Administrative and Budgetary Questions) during the 67th UN General Assembly.

Mr. Ruiz Massieu assumed his new role on January 1, 2013, with the rank of Assistant Secretary-General. This too, is the first time a Latin American has occupied this post.

The ACABQ is one of the most influential areas of the United Nations and is responsible for reviewing the budgets submitted by the UN Secretary-General for peacekeeping operations and for the operation of the UN agencies and programs.

Carlos Ruiz Massieu's appointment comes in recognition of his strong academic and professional background. He has extensive multilateral experience in development cooperation and administrative and budgetary matters. He is already working on the ACABQ, to which he was elected in 2011.

Carlos Ruiz Massieu is a member of the Mexican Foreign Service and holds a law degree from the Iberoamericana University and a Master's Degree in Political Science from the University of Essex. He has been posted to the Mexican Embassy in Costa Rica and to the Permanent Mission of Mexico to the United Nations in New York.

The Foreign Ministry reaffirms its commitment to the objectives and work of the UN and is ready to continue working on improving the organization's efficiency, effectiveness, transparency, and accountability.

Ms. Virginia Gamba, Director and Deputy of the Office for Disarmament Affairs

Ms. Virginia Gamba, Director and Deputy of the Office for Disarmament Affairs holds an MSC Degree in Strategic Studies from Aberystwyth

University, Wales and has worked as a technical advisor in the Americas, Africa, and Europe, and she is the author of forty publications on crisis prevention and nuclear proliferation. Her office oversees two multilateral conventions approaching universal membership that outlaw biological and chemical weapons. These have helped to sustain a global taboo against the existence of such weapons.

"Hope for a future world without nuclear weapons"—Twenty years ago, Belarus, Kazakhstan, and Ukraine renounced their nuclear arsenals. Director Gamba represented Secretary-General Ban Ki-moon at the event. Two decades after having renounced their nuclear weapons arsenals, Belarus, Kazakhstan, and Ukraine called upon the international community to redouble efforts towards eliminating all nuclear weapons. Abolishing all nuclear weapons is "the most ardent aspiration of mankind."

Office of High Commissioner for Refugees, Director Udo Janz

This office was established on December 14, 1950 by the United Nations General Assembly. The agency is mandated to lead and coordinate international action to protect refugees and resolve refugee problems worldwide. Its primary purpose is to safeguard the rights and well-being of refugees. It strives to ensure that everyone can exercise the right to seek asylum and find safe refuge in another Member State, with the option to return home voluntarily, integrate locally, or to resettle in a third country. It also has a mandate to help stateless people. In more than five decades, this Agency has helped tens of millions of people restart their lives. Today, a staff of some 6,600 people in more than 110 countries continues to help about 34 million persons.

Deputy Chief, UN Department of Public Information, Ms. Isolda Oca

Deputy Chief, UN Department of Public Information, Ms. Isolda Oca, who works with approximately 1500 NGOs that work with the UN, also welcomed the assembly of Rotarians. Originally from the Philippines, where her father and brother were Rotarians, Ms. Oca was very familiar with Rotary. She also outlined how Rotarians were essential in the creation of the United Nations. She noted that the unsuccessful predecessor of the UN, the League of Nations, failed because civil society was not incorporated into the organizational structure. It was a wise decision of US Presidents Franklin D. Roosevelt and Harry S. Truman to insist that Rotarians be involved in the creation of the United Nations. Article 71 of the UN charter states: "The Economic and Social Council may make suitable arrangements for consultation with nongovernmental organizations which are concerned with matters within its competence. Such arrangements may be made with international organizations and, where appropriate, with national organizations after consultation with the Member of the United Nations concerned." The PolioPlus Program could not have been possible without Article 71, Ms. Oca added. She advised Rotarians to remember that the purpose of the UN in 1945 was "not to help humanity go to heaven, but to save it from hell."

From their website:
http://www.un.org/en/sections/department-public-information/department-public-information/

DPI (The Department of Public Information) was established in 1946, by General Assembly resolution 13 (I), to promote global awareness and understanding of the work of the United Nations. DPI undertakes this goal through radio, television, print, the Internet, videoconferencing, and other media tools.

The Department reports annually on its work to the UN General Assembly's Committee on Information. The Committee, which meets once a year, is responsible for overseeing the work of DPI and for providing it guidance on policies, programs, and activities of the Department.

Director of UNESCO's New York Office, Ms. Helene-Marie Gosselin

Director of the UNESCO's New York Office, Ms. Helene-Marie Gosselin, pointed out that there still remains an estimated 781 million adults—two-thirds are women—who are unable to read and write. There are also 77 million children of primary age who are not enrolled in school and more than three-quarters of these out-of-school children live in sub-Sahara Africa and south and west Asia. Moreover, there are millions of children who are enrolled in school but do not attend regularly, and consequently do not learn to read and write.

UNESCO launched an initiative known as LIFE (Literacy Initiative for Empowerment). This initiative aims to create learning opportunities for illiterate adults in the poorest 35 countries where literacy rates are under 50% or the illiterate population is greater than 10 million.

She encouraged Rotarians to continue their local community projects as well as their international literacy projects because illiteracy is prevalent in pockets of even the most developed countries, and Rotarians have been terrific partners with such groups as Literacy Volunteers of America, as well as English as a Second Language programs.

From their website:
https://devjobsindo.org/organisations/unesco

In 1945, UNESCO was created in order to respond to the firm belief of nations, forged by two world wars in less than a generation, for which political and economic agreements are not enough to build a lasting peace. Peace must be established on the basis of humanity's moral and intellectual solidarity.

UNESCO strives to build networks among nations that enable this kind of solidarity, by:

- Mobilizing for education: so that every child, boy or girl, has access to quality education as a fundamental human right and as a prerequisite for human development.
- Building intercultural understanding: through protection of heritage and support for cultural diversity. UNESCO created the idea of World Heritage to protect sites of outstanding universal value.
- Pursuing scientific cooperation: such as early warning systems for tsunamis or transboundary water management agreements to strengthen ties between nations and societies.
- Protecting freedom of expression: an essential condition for democracy, development and human dignity.

UNAIDS (UN Program on HIV and AIDS), Dr. Ortega

UN Program on HIV and AIDS, or UNAIDS, Dr. Ortega, is the main advocate for coordinated global action on the HIV epidemic. He gave an insightful presentation of the world's fight against the spread of the infection.

As of January 2006, UNAIDS estimates that AIDS has killed more than 25 million people since it was first recognized in 1981, making it one of the most destructive epidemics in recorded history. In 2005 alone, AIDS claimed an estimated 3 million lives, of which more than 570,000 were children. A third of these deaths are occurring in sub-Saharan Africa, retarding economic growth and destroying human capital. While drug treatment reduces both the mortality and the morbidity of HIV infection, access to the necessary medication is not available in all countries. The doctor also noted that blood transfusions of unsafe or untested blood is a significant cause for the spread of AIDs.

He pointed out that UNAIDS' mission is to lead, strengthen, and support an expanded response to HIV/AIDS that includes preventing transmission, providing care and support to those already living with the virus, reducing the vulnerability of individuals and communities to HIV, and alleviating the impact of the epidemic. The doctor also emphasized that the UN is assertively seeking Civil Society engagement and the development of strategic partnerships with organizations like Rotary.

Chief of the Education Cluster at UNICEF, Mr. Cream Wright

Chief of the Education Cluster at UNICEF, Mr. Cream Wright, clarified that every child deserves an education, and that school is about more than just learning. He pointed out that UNICEF supports education programs serving children from preschool age through adolescence. Since the majority of children not in school are girls, we make a special effort to give girls a learning opportunity which transforms lives and yields spectacular benefits in social and economic development. However, Mr. Wright also pointed out that the quality of education is very important. It is essential to determine when children stay, complete school, and that they are learning.

From their website:
http://educationcluster.net

The Education Cluster is an open formal forum for coordination and collaboration on education in humanitarian crises. The Education Cluster brings together NGOs, UN Agencies, academics, and other partners under the shared goal of ensuring predictable, well-coordinated and equitable provision of education for populations affected by humanitarian crises.

Established in 2007 by the IASC (Inter-Agency Standing Committee) as part of the cluster approach, the Education Cluster works to uphold education as a basic human right and core component of humanitarian response. The Education Cluster is the only cluster co-led at global level by a UN Agency and an NGO: UNICEF and Save the Children.

Chief of UNICEF's Water, Sanitation and Hygiene Section, Ms. Clarissa Brocklehurst

Chief of UNICEF's Water, Sanitation and Hygiene Section, Ms. Clarissa Brocklehurst, spoke about the need for clean water and sanitation, although she remarked that she felt that she is speaking to the converted. UNICEF has a $245 million budget and is currently working in 90 countries with a staff of 300. Needless to say, with such a colossal task, it needs the support and assistance of organizations like Rotary. In addition, UNICEF works with the World Bank and the African Development Bank for funding major sanitation projects such as pipelines and treatment plants.

More and more, NGOs are looking at the linkages of clean water and its impact on the other Millennium Development Goals. It is now apparent that health and nutrition are related to accessing clean water. Ms. Brocklehurst pointed out that in a recent medical journal it was asserted that proper sanitation is the greatest medical milestone since1948, even more important than most medicines. For example, people with AIDS cannot successfully adhere to their treatments and remain healthy without clean water.

Sanitation also affects education. Schools have to be girl-friendly, and separate bathrooms are needed for girls or many parents will not send their girls to school. Also, time saved not carrying water from a distant well allows for more classroom time and studying. While many wells and pumps are being installed, and storage tanks for rainwater are being built thanks to Rotary and other NGOs, promotion of thorough handwashing is an important step to stop the spread of infection.

Social marketing is very effective when executed properly. Therefore, a major campaign is ongoing to encourage more handwashing. WASH partnerships with Unilever, Procter and Gamble, The Gates Foundation, and others have promoted thorough handwashing habits at the community level. When an educational campaign is effective, then the family and villages will build their own sanitation facilities, UNICEF has ascertained. She also announced that while it is still somewhat of a taboo subject in many societies, next year (2008) is the International Year for Sanitation and she proudly promoted UNICEF's "Sanitation is Beautiful" flyer. She also noted that storage of clean water is very important.

From their website:
https://www.unicef.org/wash/3942_3952.html

WASH is the collective term for Water, Sanitation and Hygiene. Due to their interdependent nature, these three core issues are grouped together to represent a growing sector. While each is a separate field of work, each is dependent on the presence of the other. For example, without toilets, water sources become contaminated; without clean water, basic hygiene practices are not possible.

United Nations Millennium Project Director, Professor Jeffrey Sachs

United Nations Millennium Project Director, Professor Jeffrey Sachs, is also the Director of the Earth Institute at Columbia University and was noted as one of the one-hundred most influential leaders in the world by *Time* magazine.

He thanked Rotarians for their work and their one hundred years of service. "Rotarians stand for what all citizens need to be, and when I give speeches around the world, I always point out to other organizations Rotary's PolioPlus Program as a model of public-private partnerships," he noted. Rotary International was the first of all organizations to understand the global mission that we have one world.

The MDGs (Millennium Developmental Goals) of 2000 are the world's shared hopes and goals. Unfortunately, they are not on track.

The MDGs are the life and death struggle for the world. Twenty to thirty thousand men, women, and especially children die every day of extreme poverty. A $7.00 anti-malaria treated mosquito net will last for five years and protect two children, yet three million will die from malaria.

> The goals are sensible and achievable, yet still bold commitments. We still have a decade to put in the practical steps in even the poorest and the most seemingly hopeless parts of the planet. In the PolioPlus Program, Rotarians did not say we are going to implement our life saving project in only parts of the planet and that some of the other countries are too poor, or hopeless, or too poorly governed to get the job done. Needless to say, if the MDGs are not achieved on schedule, it will be an embarrassment for all and "we will be a world without shared goals.

He also emphasized that we need all of the goals to be achieved since poverty has to be defined in its entirety of income, hunger, gender equality, disease control, safe childbirth, access to water and sanitation, and environmental sustainability.

The world leaders got it so right when they set the goals in 2000. "The definition of poverty is not one dollar a day; if there is no clinic, no roads, and no girls going to school, what good is one dollar a day?"

Millennium Goal villages require assistance to eliminate extreme poverty. They need:

- Donated seed and fertilizer
- Treadle pumps for water
- Schools available for male and female children
- School meals in the schools as an incentive to send their daughters, as well as their sons to the schools
- A local clinic that is stocked with oral dehydration solutions, basic antibiotics for acute respiratory infections, and anti-malaria drugs
- Mosquito nets at every sleeping site in malaria transmission regions

- Help in transport and communication of people and cargo to reduce head loading

"To provide this assistance for self-sufficiency, it will cost approximately $50 per person per year for several years to end extreme poverty in its entirety within a generation. The MDGs want to cut extreme poverty in half by 2015, but we could end extreme poverty by 2025," he said. Professor Sachs concluded his remarks by stating, "I am grateful to Rotary International for leading to achieve the Millennium Development Goals because the peace on the planet depends on them."

Deputy Executive Director of UNICEF, Rima Salah

Deputy Executive Director of UNICEF, Rima Salah, Rotary Partnerships with UNICEF, "proves that miracles do happen and they have made a better world for children." More than 2 billion children have been immunized on the PolioPlus Program public-private partnership. Rotary's comparative advantage is that Rotarians are everywhere, and Rotarians are connected to, or they are, the local decision makers to get the message out.

While nearly $4 billion has been raised, more than $600 million of this amount was contributed by Rotarians. She also credited the Vitamin A nutrients in the vaccine to have saved an estimated that 1 million children's lives.

She noted, however, because of food shortages:

- 300 million children who are malnourished
- Six million children under 5 years of age die every year
- 27% are underweight

Disappointedly, while the international community had hoped to cut the number of under-weight children in half by 2015, in the last five years the number has only been reduced by 1%.

A properly nourished a child needs:

- A healthy mother
- Exclusive breastfeeding for the first six months of life

- Breastfeeding—combined with a daily intake of high protein complimentary food from 6 months to two years of age
- Iodized salt (Kiwanis International is the led NGO with UNICEF in this area)
- Nutritious food three or four times a day from age two to five

Senior External Relations Officer at WHO, Dr. Richard Alderslade

Senior External Relations Officer at WHO, Dr. Richard Alderslade, spoke on the report "Make Every Mother and Child Count."

This report states that every year:

- Five hundred thousand women die during pregnancy or childbirth
- Four million children die during their first day of life
- Ten to twelve million children die before 5 years of age
- Sixty-eight thousand die from unsafe abortions
- Malaria causes 800,000 deaths, mostly children and mostly in Africa
- One hundred fifty million are suffering from diabetes

(For more information go to or click *http://www.who.int/whr/2005/en/index.html* and *http://www.who.int/whr/2005/overview_en.pdf*)

Five medical illnesses are responsible for the deaths of 90% of children:

1. Preterm birth respiratory infection, most notably pneumonia
2. Diarrhea
3. Malaria
4. Measles
5. HIV/AIDS

Partnerships with NGO are identified WHO website. These problems are far too large for any one organization and we need to partnership the doctor noted.

Ms. Oca noted that there is a growing force of civil society at the United Nations, and the UNDPI wants to provide assistance. While the

United Nations is not an organization of civil society, but of Member States, civil society can, and does, have a voice in the process. "Today, the United Nations stands for a world where people of different nations and cultures can look at each other, not with fear and suspicion, but as potential partners to exchange good and ideas for their mutual benefit, and civil society is a vital partner in this endeavor." In the last few years, commitment to civil society evolvement has become evident by the realignment of the UN outreach programs to engage and assist civil society.
They include:

- Recent conference titled "Our Challenge: Voices for Peace Partnership and Renewal" (Rotary was represented at this conference as well as 700 other organizations; the next conference is scheduled for September, 2006.)
- "NGO Briefings" are held every Thursday from 10:00 a.m. to 12:00 p.m. UNDPI provides the perspectives of Member States, the UN, and that of civil society on issues pending at the UN.
- Communication and Information Exchange Workshops to enhance NGOs' dissemination of information
- UNDPI library has transformed from a library of book collection to that of people connection.
- Orientation programs for new NGOs
- Commission of the Cordoza Report by the Secretary-General in 2003 that recommends future and enhanced UN interaction with Civil Society
- Establishment of NGO "Focal Points" at most UN agencies and departments
- Establishment of "Special Advisor for NGO Relations" to the President of the General Assembly
- Significant NGO input in the 2005 Outcome Document as exemplified by "No development without security, no security without development, and no security without human rights"

United Nations University in Tokyo, Momoyo Ise

Ms. Momoyo Ise, is a former officer at the Liaison Office of UNU (United

Nations University) in Tokyo, which provides professional training as well as training in six languages. Ms. Ise also headed many UN Departments during her career at the United Nations. For the last eight years, since her retirement from the UN, and the Rotary Club of New York, Ms. Ise has worked with the Asian Women's Fund in Tokyo.

From their website:
https://unu.edu/about/unu

UNU (United Nations University) is a global think tank and postgraduate teaching organization headquartered in Japan. You can learn more about the history of UNU, how the University is organized and about its current leadership.

The mission of the UN University is to contribute, through collaborative research and education, to efforts to resolve the pressing global problems of human survival, development and welfare that are the concern of the United Nations, its Peoples and Member States.

In carrying out this mission, the UN University works with leading universities and research institutes in UN Member States, functioning as a bridge between the international academic community and the United Nations System.

Through postgraduate teaching activities, UNU contributes to capacity building, particularly in developing countries.

Under-Secretary-General for Communications and Public Information, Kiyotaka Akasaka

Under-Secretary-General for Communications and Public Information, Kiyotaka Akasaka, also welcomed the Rotarians. Mr. Akasaka joined the Japanese Foreign Ministry in 1971 after graduating from Kyoto University. He held senior positions in the World Health Organization and was a member of the Secretariat of the GATT (General Agreement on Tariffs and Trade), the precursor of the World Trade Organization up until April 2007. He also held the position of Deputy Secretary-General of the OECD (Organization for Economic Cooperation and Development) where he was responsible for sustainable development, the environment, and partnership with other international organizations. He also chaired the Kyoto Protocol.

He recalled his mind-set when in 1996 he participated in one of Rotary's vaccination campaigns in Africa, and he realized that the children he had just dispensed the vaccine to will never get polio! It was a profound and inspiring feeling, and he was grateful to participate in such a noble program. He also invited Rotarians to support the 60th anniversary of the Declaration of Human Rights on December 10, 2008 in Paris, France where the original document was signed.

Dr. Melanie Renshaw, Senior Health Advisor at UNICEF's Regional Office for Eastern and Southern Africa

Dr. Melanie Renshaw, the Senior Health Advisor at UNICEF's Regional Office for Eastern and Southern Africa outlined how malaria kills a child somewhere in the world every 30 seconds. It infects 350-500 million people each year, killing 1 million, mostly children. In addition, 90% of malaria deaths occur in Africa, and malaria accounts for about one-fifth of all childhood deaths. Malaria also has serious economic impacts by slowing economic growth and development and perpetuating the vicious cycle of poverty.

The good news is that malaria is both preventable and treatable, and effective preventive practices have been implemented in many parts of the malaria-infected regions of the world. She noted that sleeping under ITNs (Insecticide Treated Nets) can reduce overall child mortality by 20%. There are studies that show ITNs, when consistently and correctly used, can save six child lives per year for every one thousand children sleeping under them.

United Nations Speaker Program, Mr. Falt of UNDPI (The United Nation's Department of Public Information)

Prior to joining the UN, Mr. Eric Falt was the Press Attaché for the Permanent Mission of France to the United Nations. Mr. Falt has been a longtime supporter of Rotary since the time he was stationed in Chicago, frequently visited clubs throughout the Midwest, and he has recognized that Rotary is an indispensable partner to the United Nations. He also pointed out the long history of Rotarians in the creation of the United

Nations, with no less than forty-nine Rotarians contributing to the twenty-nine delegations at the San Francisco Conference in 1945. The UN hopes to work even more closely with Rotarians and asks that Rotarians invite United Nations personnel to speak at organized events throughout the United States. The speakers do not accept honorarium; however, they only ask that the clubs finance travel and accommodation expenses. He also invited Rotarians to the UN's annual events around the world. The upcoming conference will be in Paris, and the year after that in Mexico with the program dealing with human rights and disarmament.

UNEP (UN Environment Programme), Tom Hamlin

At UNEP, Tom Hamlin's department has worked on alternative energy and transportation projects in more than thirty countries in the last ten years. He currently works for the UN Department of Technical and Social Affairs.

Mr. Hamlin pointed out that approximately thirty countries, representing 2.8 billion people, especially China, India, Kenya, Ethiopia, Nigeria, and Peru confront chronic water problems. Furthermore, effects from climate change can be very dramatic within the next twenty years, particularly in Africa. One projected effect is that there will be a 20% drop in available water supply, with a concomitant increase in population. There is evidence that floods and droughts are occurring more frequently and are more severely.

The tactics to moderate water shortages are:

- Seek new sources, desalinization, and reverse osmosis
- Save water, repair porous pipes, and upgrade water delivery systems
- Reduce demand, initiate water efficient farming techniques, and reduce water flow rates in faucets and toilets
- Recycle terrace farming, hierarchical, multi-uses of water, and more water treatment plants

"There are three legs to end the cycle of poverty: Health, Hunger, and Education"

WHO Visits to Update Rotarians on the PolioPlus Program

Mr. Anand Balachandran, the Interagency Coordinator of the WHO (World Health Organization), gave an update on Rotary and the PolioPlus Program. As most Rotarians are well aware, in 1985 Rotary International unilaterally embarked on the worldwide initiative to bring about a polio-free world. At the time, there were 125 countries that were polio-endemic and 350,000 children were infected every year. A few years later, the global health community joined and partnered with Rotary in 1988. He noted that Rotary's initiative has saved more than five million children from polio-inflicted disabilities by vaccinating more than two billion children. Also, what is less recognized, is that this vaccinating program prevented the deaths of an additional 1.2 million children by providing Vitamin A along with the vaccine.

However, there a few regions, in four countries, that have been elusive where the Director-General of WHO has intensified efforts. The four countries are Nigeria with over 750 cases in 2008, India with over 500 cases, Pakistan with over 100 cases, and Afghanistan with over 30 cases. As a result, since polio knows no geographic boundaries, there have been polio cases detected in Chad, Sudan, Angola, and Geneva, Switzerland due to the stubborn persistence of polio in these four countries.

While Type 1 polio (the most dangerous strain), is prevalent in only one or two states in India, there has been a disturbing outbreak in a much wider cross-section of Nigeria. "Being the largest country in Africa, Nigeria has threatened the worldwide progress on the war on polio," he said. Of the four endemic countries, Nigeria has been singled out by the United Nations as the country where they will increase efforts in their national universal immunization program. This is one of the few times a single country has been pressured by the 192 Member States of the UN, and the Secretary-General to muster the "political will."

WHO is planning steps to immunize for the Type 3 polio virus. This is a much less dangerous strain of the virus, and easier to fight. Sadly, Mr. Kalitadra, moderator of the PolioPlus Program, pointed out that a suicide bomber attacked a clearly marked United Nations convoy on September 15, 2008 in Southern Afghanistan and killed two WHO doctors together with their driver. They were on their way to provide vaccinations to children.

NGOs (NONGOVERNMENTAL ORGANIZATIONS)

An NGO (nongovernmental organization) is a not-for-profit, voluntary citizens' group, which is organized on a local, national, or international level to address issues in support of the public good. They are usually funded by donations and are run primarily by volunteers. Since the end of World War II, NGOs have had an increasing role in international development, particularly in the fields of humanitarian assistance, and poverty alleviation. The Committee on Nongovernmental Organizations was established at the United Nations in 1946 and was included in the UN Charter.

Mr. Stein Villumstad, the Deputy Secretary-General of the World Conference of Religions for Peace

Mr. Stein Villumstad, Deputy Secretary-General of the World Conference of Religions for Peace, is also Chair of the Global Coalition that works toward a UN Decade of Interreligious and Intercultural Dialogue and Cooperation for Peace. He has also worked for twenty years with Norwegian Church Aid.

Mr. Villumstad has contributed a number of articles including: "Social Reconstruction on Africa: Perspectives from Within and Without" (Action Publishers, Nairobi, 2005).

From their website:
www.rfpusa.org

Religions for Peace USA is the largest and most broadly-based representative multireligious forum in the United States, with participants from more than 50 religious communities, representing each of the major faith traditions. The organization identifies shared commitments among religious communities in the U.S., enhances mutual understanding among these communities, and facilitates collaboration to address issues of common concern.

PPAF (Public-Private Alliance Foundation), Dr. David Stillman

Dr. David Stillman, from the Public-Private Alliance Foundation, was a UN staff member. Dr. Stillman worked with intergovernmental bodies and UN agencies on development, relief, and reconstruction. Posted to Pakistan with the UN Development Program, he previously worked in Togo, Ghana, and Kenya. He holds an MA and PhD degrees in Political Science from Duke University.

The Public-Private Alliance Foundation has held three "Partners Against Poverty" meetings at the United Nations, focusing on its program areas and the Millennium Development Goals. Foundation activities are covered in the report to the UN Economic and Social Council.

The Public-Private Alliance Foundation is a not-for-profit 501(c) (3) donor-supported corporation headquartered in New York. It is associated with the United Nations and the United Nations Global Compact. It aims to reduce poverty by networking with business, government, academia, the financial community, NGOs (Nongovernmental Organizations), UN entities, and others. The Foundation helps stimulate entrepreneurship and investment for sustainable development and helps in achieving the Millennium Development Goals. It works in several program areas including agribusiness, renewable energy, health, and microfinance. Haiti, the Dominican Republic, and Madagascar are focus countries.

International Institute of Rural Construction, Mr. Isaac Bekalo

Mr. Isaac B. Bekalo, born in Ethiopia, has twenty-five years of practical experience in community and organizational development, management, and leadership. As President of IIRR (International Institute of Rural Construction), Mr. Bekalo takes a lead role in strategy formulation, organizational diagnoses and restructuring, strategic management, business plan development, and monitoring and evaluation.

Mr. Bekalo's academic qualifications include a Doctoral Degree in Organizational Development and Planning. While pursuing his doctoral studies, he worked as a part-time lecturer in the school of Public Health and as Coordinator of Graduate Research Programs in the Philippines.

Mr. Bekalo joined IIRR in September 1989 as the Africa Regional Director and was appointed as the 6th President of IIRR in January 2009. He built IIRR's Africa Regional Center from scratch by mobilizing resources, building strong teams, and establishing a presence in four East African countries. As President, he is a voting but non-independent member of the Board of Trustees, which he was appointed to in January 2009 when he assumed the role of President. IIRR has over 80 years of history in participatory, integrated, and people-centered development. The Institute has enhanced the capacity and confidence of over 100,000 development managers, practitioners, and community leaders across Asia, Africa, and Latin America and has a long history of documenting and disseminating field-based experience through its publications. Behind this tremendous body of work is a compelling and revolutionary individual.

American Council on Africa, Dr. Sekou Koureissy Condé

Rotarian, and Executive Director of the newly established ACA (American Council on Africa), Dr. Sekou Koureissy Condé, pointed out that since 1989, at the end of Cold War, Western governments focused on initiatives to promote democratic development in Africa.

At that time, Dr. Condé was instrumental in creating a political party in Guinea that focused on peacebuilding through human rights, tolerance, and community development. He spent ten years working with local village leaders and emphasized the importance of involving them in the peace development process. In 1996, Dr. Condé was appointed Interior Secretary and Interim Foreign Minister in Guinea. Since 2002 he has lived in New York and currently teaches at Columbia University.

Dr. Condé also emphasized that he envisions that Africans learn the American model of business management to bring about development; and that Americans learn African methods of tolerance and conflict resolution. The ACA is committed to:

- Identifying, promoting, and supporting locally-generated methods and practices to prevent and peacefully resolve conflict in Africa
- Facilitating partnerships between American and African universities, secondary schools, Civil Society, and other NGOs
- Collecting, preserving, and publishing information about past and current conflicts in Africa

Mrs. Sally ("Salwa") Kader, President and Founder of USFMEP

Mrs. Sally ("Salwa") Kader, President and Founder of USFMEP (US Federation for Middle East Peace), is a global peace advocate who tirelessly works to build bridges between the United States and the Arab and Muslim worlds. Mrs. Kader is a well-known and respected public speaker in topics of interfaith dialogue, human rights, youth empowerment, and women's rights. She has spoken at the UN headquarters and across the continental United States, in Europe and throughout the Middle East, to a wide variety of audiences. She has traveled internationally to lead peace conferences and forums emphasizing the importance of mutual respect and better understanding of the Middle East including its religious philosophies, cultures, history, and political landscape.

USFMEP is a nonprofit, organization, which promotes the United Nations commitment to international peace, security, and justice through educational programs, public relations, and community outreach initiatives. Its goal is to promote understanding of Middle Eastern culture through seminars, workshops, roundtables, and public forums. It has established networks and liaison offices in other regions of the world to help raise awareness on issues concerning peace in the Middle East, utilizing the latest methods in information technology.

"The Status of the Negotiations on the Iran Nuclear Program" *By Zweites Deutsches Fernsehen, ZDF, (German Television Station)*

Mr. Klaus Prömpers, Director of the German Television, commented on the new German Government in the making. Mr. Prömpers was born February 11, 1949 in Düsseldorf, and studied economics in Cologne, Germany. He has held a number of distinguished positions including: 1976-79, Secretary-General of Catholic Youth Organization; 1980-89 Moderator and Reporter, Deutschlandfunk, Cologne, Germany; November 1989-August 1999 Reporter, Bonn, Germany, for TV ZDF (Zweites Deutsches Fernsehen); September 1999-February 2004, Brussels ZDF, March 2004-June 2011 Vienna ZDF, Balkans Bureau Chief; and since July 2011, New York ZDF Bureau Chief.

Also, more than thirty Manhattan Rotaractors attended this meeting from the Rotaract Clubs of the United Nations, Columbia University.

The New York Sun Reporter Views: What is New, and What is Not at the UN?

On January 1, 2007, Mr. Ban Ki-moon of the Republic of Korea was sworn in as the eighth Secretary-General of the United Nations. He brings to his post 37 years of service, both in government and on the global stage. Our guest speaker, Mr. Benny Avni, is a staff reporter for the New York Sun and writes often about the United Nations. Mr. Avni was born in Israel and served in the Israeli military. The New York Sun is a contemporary five-day daily newspaper published in New York City. When it debuted on April 16, 2002, it became "the first general interest broad sheet newspaper to be launched in New York in two generations."

Mr. Avni noted that Mr. Ban Ki-moon is significantly different from his predecessors regarding his relations with the United States. Experience shows that every time the United Nations clashes with the United States, the UN becomes irrelevant. Without strong cooperation with the United States, the United Nations cannot make a difference. While China is a growing power and player at the UN, and terrorist groups can have a significant capability to wreak havoc throughout the world, the United States is in fact the only superpower. As a result, the United States is able to act in the world theater—maybe not as effectively as with the UN.

"However, the UN cannot act at all without the full participation and cooperation of the United States," Mr. Avni noted. He went on to say that many UN Member States, including many of the democracies, believe that the role of the UN should be a counterweight to the United States.

For example, Boutros Boutros-Ghali entered office as "Pro-Soviet" and converted to a "Pro-United States" position. However, he began to assert UN independence, and as a result he clashed with the Clinton administration. Consequently, he was not selected by the Security Council for a customary second five-year term. The most recent Secretary-General, Kofi Annan, when selected, was very "Pro-United States," but as a consequence of his claims that the Iraq War was illegal, Mr. Annan spent the last few years of his term in confrontation with the United States.

Secretary-General Ban Ki-moon however, is of the generation that feels South Korea owes its very existence to the United States. He believes, as does our guest speaker, that the United States is a force of good in the world, and his sensibilities coincide with those of the US delegation. In addition, he also has a broader business background than his predecessors, Unlike Kofi Annan, who spent most of his career at the UN rising through its bureaucracy, Mr. Ban was a South Korean foreign minister and earned a living in the private sector. He also believes that civic work is important. Secretary-General Ban readily filled a financial disclosure form, while his predecessor was very hesitant to do so, even though all other high-level administrators and appointees at the UN were required to do so.

Furthermore, to the chagrin of our guest speaker, Mr. Ban held his first meetings at the UN in New York at 8:00 a.m. Our guest speaker and many in the UN community are not accustomed to attending meetings and briefings until lunch time. This is part of the new work ethic that Mr. Ban is trying to implement.

What is not new?

To actually change the organization's culture, Mr. Ban had to bring in innovative, high-level administrators. However, he quickly learned that every change he attempted to make had to navigate through a massive mill to be accepted by the bureaucracy. Then the changes ultimately had to be approved by the General Assembly. In order to make some transformations, Secretary-General Ban was required to identify the "troublemakers," recompense them in some manner, and only then was he able to move forward with his adaptation. As a consequence, many of the UN high-level administrators are still in charge of many UN agencies.

Our speaker also noted that there has been much "fanfare" about the recently restructured Human Rights Council that replaced the discredited Human Rights Commission. Mr. Avni outlined the "significant" reform that was made. The reformed Council now has 48 members instead of the previous 53. He also noted that since its inception, the Human Rights Council has implemented a total of eight resolutions. All eight were regarding violations by the state of Israel, and three more are pending on Israel. *The New York Sun*'s reporter sarcastically noted that according to the newly "reformed Council," there are no other human rights violations in the world. As such Burma, Tibet, Darfur, etc., have not committed any human rights violations. Mr. Avni said that in all fairness, it should be mentioned that the reformed Council has taken "bold" steps to investigate the situation in Darfur. He also noted that Sudan is not mentioned.

Ban Ki-moon of the Republic of Korea, Official Biography from the UN website:
https://en.wikipedia.org/wiki/Ban_Ki-moon

Ban Ki-moon, born 13 June 1944) is a South Korean diplomat who was the eighth Secretary-General of the United Nations from January 2007 to December 2016. Before becoming Secretary-General, Ban was a career diplomat in South Korea's Ministry of Foreign Affairs and in the United Nations. He entered diplomatic service the year he graduated from university, accepting his first post in New Delhi, India.

Ban was the foreign minister of South Korea from January 2004 to November 2006. In February 2006 he began to campaign for the office of Secretary-General. Ban was initially considered to be a long shot for the office. As foreign minister of South Korea, however, he was able to travel to all the countries on the United Nations Security Council, a maneuver that turned him into the campaign's front runner.

On 13 October 2006, he was elected to be the eighth Secretary-General by the United Nations General Assembly. On 1 January 2007, he succeeded

Kofi Annan. As Secretary-General, he was responsible for several major reforms on peacekeeping and UN employment practices. Diplomatically, Ban has taken particularly strong views on global warming, pressing the issue repeatedly with U.S. President George W. Bush, and on the Darfur conflict, where he helped persuade Sudanese president Omar al-Bashir to allow peacekeeping troops to enter Sudan.

Ban was named the world's 32nd most powerful person by the Forbes list of The World's Most Powerful People in 2013, the highest among South Koreans. In 2014, he was named the third most powerful South Korean after Lee Kun-hee and Lee Jae-yong. In 2016, Foreign Policy named Ban one of the Top 100 Global Thinkers for his achievement of making the Paris Agreement a legally binding treaty less than a year after it was adopted.

"Reach Out and Read," Ms. Benita Somerfield, Executive Director of the Barbara Bush Foundation for Family Literacy

Ms. Benita Somerfield, Executive Director of the Barbara Bush Foundation for Family Literacy also serves as an advisor to "Reach Out and Read, and was named International Literacy Resource Person for UNESCO's "Decade of Literacy." Since 1989 Ms. Somerfield wanted to thank Rotarians for their support of the Barbra Bush Foundation around the United States buying books, providing transportation, or providing a site for the reading programs around the country.

She outlined UNESCO's groundbreaking initiative, LIFE (Literacy Initiative for Empowerment). Thirty-four countries have been identified as most needy. Local governments will drive the initiative with private partnerships. UNESCO hopes that Rotary will be part of this project.

From their website:
https://greatnonprofits.org/org/barbara-bush-foundation-for-family-literacy

The Barbara Bush Foundation for Family Literacy is focused on fulfilling its mission by providing low-income families across the nation with scholarships to learn together. We partner with a network of high-performing local family literacy programs that help both young children and their parents learn how to read and write. When families share a love of reading, children have a far greater chance to live more productive and healthier lives, graduate from high school, and obtain a better job. Supporting family literacy programs is a win-win for parents and children where they acquire basic literacy skills that help them advance their education and provide greater opportunities to succeed.

New York Rotarian, Mikio Tajima, PhD, Executive Director of Conflict Prevention NGO "Reconciliation 21"

New York Rotarian, Dr. Mikio Tajima, the Executive Director of Conflict Prevention NGO "Reconciliation 21" spoke briefly about his recent mission in Nepal. The king dismissed the country's government on February 1, 2006 because he was dissatisfied with the government's results in battling the Maoist insurgents. He held consultations with a number of potential actors in the conflict. The situation is still unsettled. Dr. Tajima outlined how the international community might assist, if and when national consensus might evolve one day in favor of holding peace talks outside Nepal. In this connection, the Japanese government has been urged to offer a site for possible peace talks

The Times of London Reporter Gives Analysis of the Immediate Future of the UN

The guest speaker at the May 18th International Breakfast Meeting was James Bone, the UN Correspondent for *The Times of London*. Mr. Bone received his degree in law from Cambridge, England and earned a Master's Degree in International Affairs and a second Master's Degree in Journalism at Columbia University. He manned the foreign desk in Rome and London before his current assignment. He also happens to be the neighbor of our own New York Rotarian and International Breakfast Meeting coordinator, Joe Klee, on the eastern end of Long Island. He spoke about the immediate future of the United Nations in light of the Oil-For-Food scandal and the possible stalemate of the recently introduced "Larger Freedom" United Nations reform package.

To start off the discussion, Mr. Bone recounted that in order to reduce the humanitarian hardship of the 1991 Gulf War trade embargo, the UN instituted an Oil-For-Food Program in 1996, where Iraq could sell some of its of oil to finance food, medicine, and other humanitarian supplies purchases. All the revenue, (approximately $64 billion), from the sale of oil came back in food, clothing, medical supplies, and also paid for the weapons inspection. However, Saddam Hussein, a genius at being able to corrupt people, proudly devised a very clever scheme to allow influential politicians, officials, and journalists to benefit from the estimated thirty cents per barrel commission on hundreds of millions of barrels of oil. Mr. Bone assured us that he never received any of these lucrative offers from Saddam Hussein.

He pointed out that the Oil-For-Food scandal is hydralike and very complex. In a nutshell, there are two main sides to the scandal: the oil sales and the humanitarian items purchases.

The first section, "Freedom from Want," outlines specific responsibilities as outlined in the Monterrey Agreement of March 2002 between the developed and developing countries. Secretary-General Annan is asking the political leaders of developing economies to improve their governance and make space for civilized society (e.g., Rotary Clubs) and the private sector to play their full part. He is also asking for duty-free and quota-free market access to all exports from the least developed countries. And most importantly, the report asks that all developed countries commit themselves to spending 0.7 per cent of their gross domestic product on official development assistance.

The second section, titled "Freedom from Fear," is asking for Member States to commit themselves to work together to deter terrorism, civil wars, deadly weapons proliferation, and to establish a Peacebuilding Commission.

The third section, "Freedom to Live in Dignity," asks Member States to strengthen the rule of law, human rights, and democracy.

Finally, the last section, "Strengthening the United Nations" is asking the Security Council membership to be more representative of the geopolitical realities of today. The report is also proposing that the Economic and Security Council play the leading role in implementing coherent United Nations policies on development. In addition, it recommends the creation of a new Human Rights Council to replace the discredited Commission on Human Rights.

Mr. Bone noted that there are many obstacles to the reform package.

The expansion of the Security Council from 15 to 25 members proposes to give Germany, Japan, India, and Brazil permanent seats. Furthermore, the new permanent members would have the same responsibilities and obligations as the current permanent members, including veto power over Security Council resolutions. But any change requires two-thirds support from the 191 Member States, and cannot be vetoed by any of the five current members of the Security Council. Unfortunately, China has already taken firm position against Japanese membership in the Security Council (Japan's financial support of the UN is second only to the United States). On other issues, such as a definition of terrorism, some Arab nations are starting to back away.

As is normally the case in all organizations, there is a greater constituency to prevent change than for change to occur. As a result, in Mr. Bone's opinion, it is unlikely that there will be major changes introduced at the summit in September. The Peacebuilding Proposal that would oversee post-conflict areas has a good chance of passage, however.

"Reach Out and Read," Carmen Ramos-Bonoan, MD

Carmen Ramos-Bonoan, MD, a pediatrician and a native of the Philippines, is the National Director of ROR (Reach Out and Read) in the Philippines. Dr. Ramos-Bonoan is also very familiar with Rotary because her husband has been a longtime Rotarian. Started in 1989 in Boston by a concerned group of pediatricians, ROR encourages literacy promotion as a standard part of pediatric primary care so that children will grow up with books and a love of reading. Doctors, nurses, and other health-care providers advise parents about the importance of reading aloud, and give age-appropriate books to children at pediatric checkups from six months to five years of age. By building on the unique relationship between parents and medical providers, ROR helps families and communities encourage early literacy skills so children enter school prepared for success in reading. This program has helped more than three million children. Dr. Ramos-Bonoan concluded her presentation informing the attendees that with the help of the United Nations and Rotary, "We can eliminate illiteracy."

From their website:
http://www.reachoutandread.org/about-us

Reach Out and Read is a nonprofit organization that gives young children a foundation for success by incorporating books into pediatric care and encouraging families to read aloud together.

The Reach Out and Read evidence-based program builds on the unique relationship between parents and medical providers to develop critical early reading skills in children, beginning in infancy. As recommended by the American Academy of Pediatrics, Reach Out and Read incorporates early literacy into pediatric practice, equipping parents with tools and knowledge to ensure that their children are prepared to learn when they start school.

Reach Out and Read serves nearly 4.5 million children and their families annually. Reach Out and Read families read together more often, and their children enter kindergarten with larger vocabularies and stronger language skills. During the preschool years, children served by Reach Out and Read score three to six months ahead of their non-Reach Out and Read peers on vocabulary tests. These early foundational language skills help start children on a path of success when they enter school.

UN Global Compact in the Americas, Africa, and the Middle East, Mr. Jonas Haertle

Mr. Jonas Haertle, who was asked to fill in as a guest speaker the night before the conference, is a Senior Advisor and Local Network Coordinator for the United Nations Global Compact in the Americas, Africa, and the Middle East. The UN Global Compact is a strategic policy initiative for businesses that are committed to aligning their operations and strategies with ten universally accepted principles in the areas of human rights, labor, environment and anti-corruption. By doing so, business, as a primary agent driving globalization, can help ensure that markets, commerce, technology, and finance advance in ways that benefit economies and societies everywhere.

The ten principles are:

1. Support and respect the protection of internationally proclaimed human rights
2. Make sure that they are not complicit in human rights abuses

3. Uphold the freedom of association and the effective recognition of the right to collective bargaining
4. Eliminate all forms of forced and compulsory labor
5. Promote effective abolition of child labor
6. Eliminate discrimination in respect of employment and occupation
7. Support a precautionary approach to environmental challenges
8. Undertake initiatives to promote greater environmental responsibility
9. Encourage the development and diffusion of environmentally friendly technologies
10. Work against corruption in all its forms, including extortion and bribery

Public Health Nutrition Official in UNIEF Headquarters, Dr. Ian Darnton-Hill

Public Health Nutrition Official in UNIEF Headquarters, Dr. Ian Darnton-Hill, a physician in New York, stressed that hunger alleviation is the underpinning base of all development programs for UN agencies and partnerships. Eight hundred fifty million people suffer from hunger and additional an additional one hundred thirty-five million have been significantly affected by this year's price rise of food staples. There are six to eight countries in Sub-Sahara Africa and South Asia where the situation has gotten worse. Sixty-four countries are on target, but fifty-one countries are not making progress, and there are twenty-four countries that have a chronic shortage of food. Work is still needed to improve breastfeeding, diarrhea and parasite control, treat severe malnutrition, and improve household food security.

Additional effort is needed for women during pregnancy and the child's first two years of life. If a child is malnourished for more than the first two years of life, the damage is probably irreversible. While more than a third of all child deaths in developing countries are from malnutrition, for those that survive, "it blunts their intellect, saps the productivity of everyone it touches, and perpetuates poverty."

Although fewer children are undernourished than they were ten years ago, over one hundred forty million children in the developing world are still underweight. Significant progress has also been made in relation to Vitamin A supplementation, thanks to Rotary's PolioPlus Program. However, micronutrient (essential vitamin and mineral intake) deficiencies remain significant public health problems in many countries.

UNICEF needs partners such as Rotary committed to scale up and sustain the current high-impact nutrition interventions in areas such as Infant and Young Child Feeding, Micronutrient Nutrition, Household Food Security in Emergencies, and Nutrition and HIV/AIDS.

As many already know, Rotary has a long history with the United Nations. In fact, many Rotarians were active participants in the UN creation and were original signers to the UN Charter. In a letter to commemorate the Rotary Day at the United Nations 2006 outgoing Secretary-General of the United Nations Kofi Annan wrote:

> *For more than 100 years, Rotary has been at the forefront of efforts to improve the lives of people around the world. And, since the United Nations was created, Rotary has been a wonderful partner to us. You have joined forces with us in efforts for health, literacy, and poverty eradication. You have spread the word about the work of the United Nations. You have promoted peace through your exchange programs. And, you have played a critical and historic role in our joint mission to eradicate polio worldwide.*
>
> *Rotary is living proof that people with diverse backgrounds can learn to get along with each other and concentrate more on the things we have in common, rather than on the things that drive us apart. That is what our humanitarian work is all about.*
>
> *This is the last time I will be writing to you as Secretary-General of the United Nations. So, this is the time to thank all of you for the wonderful support you have given me and the Organization for the past ten years. Thank you for understanding that this is your United Nations. Thank you for understanding that it is up to all of us to make the*

most of this indispensable instrument in the interests of the people it exists to serve.

The Earth Institute, Dr. Roberto Lenton

The Earth Institute, Dr. Roberto Lenton,—Secretary-General Kofi Annan's advisory organization on the Millennium Development Goals outlined that clean and safe water was essential to human life. Yet, over one billion people lack clean, safe drinking water, and over two billion lack access to hygienic sanitation. These two facts allow water and airborne, preventable diseases to claim six thousand lives daily around the world—the majority of them being children. In addition, in many villages, water may be two to three miles away. Too often, women and children have to carry up to forty pounds of water on their backs and too often the water is unsafe to drink.

In addition, providing more clean water can enhance the progress of many of the MDGs. For example:

- Health—Healthy people can better help themselves.
- Hunger—Illness from unsafe water brings caloric loss and hunger.
- Education—Hours not spent getting water can be spent in school.
- Environment—Less pressure on fresh water supplies

Water is Life, L'Eau, C'est La Vie, Aman Iman

Aman Iman, Director, Water is Life explained recent droughts have pushed millions of Niger's people who depend on rainwater to sustain crops and livestock to the brink of starvation. Two-thirds of Niger's surface is covered by the Sahel desert, which limits its people from migrating to more fertile grounds within their country.

The Nomad Foundation

Rotarians from District 1030 (England) set up the West Africa Trust to support projects in Niger. In addition, a US-based nonprofit, joined the new Rotary Club of Agadez and teamed up with US Rotarians on a new RI Matching Grant project. Belgian and German Rotarians are working on a number of RI Matching Grant Projects, partnering with Niger Rotarians and UNICEF to build wells. Rotarians worldwide have contributed more than $700,000 for humanitarian efforts in Niger last year, much of it for long-term, sustainable aid that will help end the cycle of poverty.

World Federalist Movement, William Pace, Executive Director

William Pace, Executive Director of the World Federalist Movement, considered by many as one of the leading experts in NGO and UN partnerships, pointed out that the United States contributes approximately $4 billion a year to the UN System or about $13 per capita; Norway contributes approximately $125 per capita, Netherlands $45, France $18, and Canada contributes $8 per capita. Compared to all levels of government spending on national, state, and local levels where total government spending in the United States is approximately $20,000 per person, relatively very little spending is done at the international, or global level. As such, with increasing responsibilities and challenges, including poverty eradication, environmental degradation, terrorism, peacekeeping, etc., the UN needs to tap the resources and the expertise available from NGOs and Civil Society.

The World Federalist Movement, once headed by Sir Peter Ustinov, is an international citizen's movement working for justice, peace, and sustainable prosperity. They lobby for an end to the rule of force, through a world governed by law, based on strengthened and democratized world institutions. World federalists support the creation of democratic global structures accountable to the citizens of the world and call for the division of international authority among separate agencies.

CONGO (The Conference of NGOs) in Consultative Relationship with the United Nations, Jackie Shapiro

Ms. Jackie Shapiro outlined the work of her organization CONGO (The Conference of NGOs) in Consultative Relationship with the United Nations. For more than 50 years, CONGO has been actively promoting the involvement of NGOs in working with the United Nations, especially in developing countries, and in achieving the UN's Millennium Goals. It currently represents more than 500 NGOs.

As stated on their website,
http://www.ngocongo.org/

CONGO assists a variety of NGOs in a consultative status to promote their common aim of supporting the United Nations Charter. It also provides a forum for nongovernmental organizations with common interests to come together to study, plan, support, and act in relation to the principles and programs of the United Nations.

As defined by the UNDPI (United Nations Department of Public Information), an NGO (Nongovernmental Organization) is any nonprofit voluntary citizens' group which is organized on a local, national, or international level. Task-oriented and driven by people with a common interest, NGOs perform a variety of services and humanitarian functions, bring citizens' concerns to Governments, monitor policies, and encourage political participation at the community level. They provide analysis and expertise, serve as early warning mechanisms, and help monitor and implement international agreements. Some are organized around specific issues, such as human rights, the environment, or health. Their relationship with offices and agencies of the United Nations System differs depending on their goals, venue, and mandate.

Historically, NGOs with consultative status are divided into three organization categories:

1. Those with a basic interest in most of the activities of the Council
2. Those which have a special competence in, and are concerned specifically with, only a few of the Council's fields of activity
3. Those which have a significant contribution to make to the work of the Council which may be placed on a register for ad hoc consultations

NGOs applying for association with UNDPI should satisfy the following requirements:

- Must support and respect the principles of the Charter of the United Nations
- Must have a recognized national or international standing

- Operate solely on a non-for-profit basis and have tax-exempt status
- Must have the commitment and the means to conduct effective information programs with its constituents and to a broader audience regarding UN activities by publishing newsletters, bulletins, and pamphlets, organizing conferences, seminars and roundtables, or enlisting the attention of the media
- Have an established record of continuity of work for a minimum of three years and should show promise of sustained activity in the future
- Have a satisfactory record of collaboration with UN Information Centers/Services or other parts of the UN System prior to association
- Provide an audited annual financial statement, conducted by a qualified independent accountant
- Have statutes/bylaws providing a transparent process for taking decisions and elections of officers and members of the Board of Directors.

Asian Peace and People's Fund for Women

The purpose of the Asian Peace and People's Fund for Women, AWF (Asian Women's Fund) is to make atonement from the Japanese people to the former "Comfort Women," and to try to "solve today's problems regarding women's honor and dignity" by enlightening people in Japan and overseas about the importance of protecting women. The AWF promotes activities aimed at "building an international society in which such conduct shall never be repeated."

"Wartime Comfort Women," refers to non-Japanese, Asian women who were forced to provide sexual services during World War II to the Japanese military. In 1990, a citizen of the Republic of Korea, and a former "Comfort Woman," addressed the Japanese Government Assembly and demanded that Japan acknowledge responsibility. As a result, the Japanese government conducted two full-scale inquiries in 1992 and 1993 that documented the involvement of the Japanese military in behavior that "... severely injured the honor and dignity of many women."

WFP (World Food Programme), Deborah Saidy, the New York Director

The New York Director of WFP (World Food Programme), Deborah Saidy, is a graduate of American University in Washington D.C. and earned an undergraduate degree from Smith College. She joined the UN in 1992 and previously served as the Emergency Coordinator for World Food Programme in Johannesburg.

She noted that the WFP strives to eradicate hunger and malnutrition, with the ultimate goal of eliminating the need for food aid itself. Yet on any given day, the WFP has twenty planes in the air and five thousand trucks on the ground. She emphasized that the development of agriculture in key troublesome regions is the long-term solution to alleviate global hunger.

The core strategies behind WFP activities, according to its mission statement, are to provide food aid to:

- Save lives in refugee and other emergency situations
- Improve the nutrition and quality of life of the most vulnerable people at critical times in their lives
- Help build assets and promote the self-reliance of poor people and communities, particularly through labor-intensive works programs
- Help the chronic poor—25,000 people die every day, and many are susceptible to malaria and tuberculosis

One China and One Taiwan Policy, Professor Lung-chu Chen

"One China and One Taiwan" policy advocate, Professor Lung-chu Chen, received his Doctor of the Science of Law Degree from Yale University and is Chairman of the Taiwan New Century Foundation. Professor Chen is also a Professor of Law at New York Law School and President of the Taiwan United Nations Alliance. He announced that he was proud to be among fellow Rotarians. Professor Chen was a Rotarian in Orange, Connecticut, USA, and Charter President of Taipei Far East Rotary Club. He proudly reported that there are more than one hundred Rotary Clubs in Taipei.

> *The One-China policy refers to the policy or view that there is only one state called "China," despite the existence of two governments that claim to be "China." As a policy, this means that countries seeking diplomatic relations with the PRC (People's Republic of China)—Mainland China must break official relations with the ROC (Republic of China)—Taiwan and vice versa.*

The Professor outlined his concern regarding the injustice of excluding Taiwan from the United Nations. "There are 192 countries in the world and Taiwan is the only country that is not a member of the United Nations." As a democratic, economically prosperous, country of 23 million people, Taiwan wants to be a member of the community of nations. "We are not asking for membership as a representative of all of China, but as the ROC independent state of Taiwan," he noted. Political reality is that Taiwan exists as an independent state and is a separate country from the People's Republic of China. The "One China" policy needs to be restated as the "One China and One Taiwan" policy.

The ROC (Republic of China)—Taiwan was a member of the United Nations until 1971. However, because of PRC (People's Republic of China)—Mainland China pressure and the United States improving relations with the PRC during the early 1970s, the United Nations General Assembly approved Resolution 2758 recognizing the PRC as the only lawful representative of China in the United Nations and its related organizations.

Resolution 2758: Restoration of the Lawful Rights of the People's Republic of China in the United Nations

> *The General Assembly,*
>
> *Recalling the principles of the Charter of the United Nations,*
>
> *Considering the restoration of the lawful rights of the People's Republic of China is essential both for the protection of the Charter of the United Nations and for the cause that the United Nations must serve under the Charter,*

> *Recognizing that the representatives of the Government of the People's Republic of China are the only lawful representatives of China to the United Nations and that the People's Republic of China is one of the five permanent members of the Security Council,*
>
> *Decides to restore all its rights to the People's Republic of China and to recognize the representatives of its Government as the only legitimate representatives of China to the United Nations, and to expel forthwith the representatives of Chiang Kai-shek from the place which they unlawfully occupy at the United Nations and in all the organizations related to it.*

1967th plenary meeting, #25 October 1971

While many Member States supported the 1971 resolution recognizing the PRC as the only lawful representative of China, Professor Chen clearly pointed out that the PRC had itself only been in existence since 1949 and that it has never ruled Taiwan for a single day. Taiwan and China have divergent political, economic, social and cultural systems, and are two independent states.

Historical Background

Following China's defeat in the first Sino-Japanese War in 1895, China ceded Taiwan to Japan in perpetuity. However, while Japan spent the next 50 years attempting to make Taiwan part of its empire, Japan's rule of Taiwan came to an end with its defeat in World War II in 1945.

In 1949, with the end of the Chinese civil war between the (KMT) Kuomintang and the Chinese Communists, the ROC administration, led by Chiang Kai-shek, was exiled to Taiwan. In the San Francisco Peace Treaty with Japan and the Peace Treaty between the ROC and Japan, both of which came into force in 1952, Japan formally renounced all rights, claims, and title to Taiwan.

However, the treaties failed to determine the beneficiary state upon Japan's renunciation. As such, Taiwan's legal status remained undefined, but was expected at the time to be settled through the United Nations in the near future.

The question of "Chinese Representation" at the United Nations was left to be addressed by the General Assembly. Unfortunately, "The Moratorium Formula," which was implemented whenever the situation was put before the General Assembly, postponed a decision year after year. This postponement cycle lasted until the early 1960s when many former African and Asian colonies acquired UN membership. During this time, the new Member States inherited the conundrum of supporting the ROC which represented China at the UN. Member States did not have access to the mainland, or the ability to support the PRC, which had control of the mainland, but was denied UN membership.

Another delaying tactic at the time, Professor Chen outlined, was the "Important Question Formula," which stipulated that any decision regarding Chinese Representation required a two-thirds majority from the General Assembly, and thereby further delayed any action on this issue.

Until 1987, Resolution 2758 was not openly questioned by the Taiwanese people primarily because Taiwan was under "martial law," and its citizens could not protest the fact that they were international orphans. However, by 1993, Taiwan had attempted to gain entry into the United Nations under joint proposals sponsored by countries friendly to Taiwan, considering among other things, Article 4 of the UN Charter.

United Nations Charter—Article 4 states:

1. Membership in the United Nations is open to all other peace-loving states, which accept the obligations contained in the present Charter, and in the judgment of the Organization, are able and willing to carry out these obligations.
2. The admission of any such state to membership in the United Nations will be effected by a decision of the General Assembly upon the recommendation of the Security Council.

Each year, since 1993, the government of Taiwan has asked friendly Member States to submit a proposal. Paradoxically, only mostly small, developing nations in Africa, Central America, and the Pacific Islands region have official diplomatic relations with the Republic of China, while many of the larger, more powerful countries, such as the United

States and the United Kingdom have de facto embassies in Taiwan. The United States, for example, maintains unofficial diplomatic relations through the American Institute in Taiwan. Taiwan's de facto embassies are referred to as "Taipei Economic and Cultural Representative Offices," and the equivalent of consulates are called "Taipei Economic and Cultural Offices."

The main reasons the United Nations Should support Taiwan membership are:

- UN Principle of Universal Participation—without Taiwan the UN does not represent the whole world and all humankind.
- Fundamental Human Rights—Taiwan should have their voice heard by the world community and would enhance the peace and security of the Asian Pacific.
- Share the "Taiwan Experience" with other Member States—not only economic development but the development of the universal values of democracy, freedom, and human rights.
- Taiwan would actively contribute financially and otherwise to the UN.

What Steps Should Be Taken?

- Member States must support the discussion of Taiwan on the merits, not on what the PRC demands.
- Acceptance of "One China and One Taiwan Policy"
- The government of Taiwan needs to push for membership under Article 4, in addition to support of Allies.
- Inform the world community that excluding Taiwan from the UN is a grave injustice.

Director, Millennium Campaign, Salil Shetty

Salil Shetty, a native of India, joined the United Nations in 2003 as the Director of the Millennium Campaign. Mr. Shetty, prior to joining the UN, was the Chief Executive of Action Aid, a leading international development NGO in South Asia and Sub-Sahara Africa. He provided an assessment of the progress as of the halfway point of the Millennium Development Goals.

He noted that some regions, particularly China and India, have made significant progress, especially in the first goal of eradicating poverty and hunger. In addition, the world has made advances with much of the crippling debts being canceled, and forty-million more children going to school. Overall, he noted that on the global level, it is likely that we'll reach the universal target of halving extreme poverty by 2015.

Yet, he emphasized that these goals are not about aggregates; they are about the people of individual countries. He pointed out that there are still huge difficulties in Sub-Saharan Africa and many countries in South Asia and are not likely to reach the goals. Also, he specified that in some parts of Latin America, things are not as successful as the numbers may indicate because of the high degree of income disparities in many of the countries with a large indigenous population.

There is concern that even though the world has made strong and sustained progress in reducing extreme poverty; this is now being undercut by recent higher prices of food, oil, and the global economic slowdown.

Mr. Shetty's department at the UN organized more than 115 million people around the world to "Stand Up and Take Action" on October 17, 2008 They were also encouraged to remind their political leaders that they expect them to deliver on the commitments made in 2000 to achieve the Millennium Development Goals. While the global movement in support of the Millennium Development Goals is growing due to the involvement of famous film actors and musicians, more assistance is needed.

Our speaker also noted that the Doha Development Rounds, which are the current trade negotiation talks at the UN WTO (World Trade Organization) needs to allow developing economies to sell their competitive products to industrialized countries without imposed trade barriers. The most recent round of negotiations in July 2008 broke down after failing to reach a compromise on agricultural import rules.

THE ROTARIAN PROJECTS

*R**otary International**, also an official NGO of the United Nations, is a worldwide service organization that was established in 1905. Its purpose is to provide an enjoyable platform for business and professional leaders to encourage high ethical standards in all vocations and to advance goodwill and peace around the world. There are approximately 34,000 clubs worldwide, and 1.2 million members.*

Full Page Advertisement from 1918: "What is Rotary?"

(The Rotary Club of New York purchased a full page advertisement in *The New York Times* in 1918, which stated: These leaders of industry offered this advertisement to the public as an expression of sincerity in business and community betterment.)

A Rotary Club is an organization of businessmen bound together with the understanding that they can better life and conditions in the community. Primarily the idea was to stimulate interchange of business among members, but this proved provincial and has long been discontinued. Today Rotary stands for the highest ideals in business and social life with benefit to all and favoritism to none.

There are 888 clubs in the same number of cities throughout the United States, Canada, Great Britain, and Cuba. The movement started in

1905, and today there are 86,806 Rotarians, each pledged to an unselfish duty. The Rotary Club of New York has 412 members, each representing a different specialization of business or profession. By virtue of its membership principles, Rotary cannot be dominated by a single selfish direction, but must serve the greatest number fearlessly and trustily..

Rotarians are in business to serve. If you go to one of the advertisers shown on the full page advertisement or purchase their merchandise, you are assured full value, courtesy, and no misrepresentation.

Gift of Life International, Grace Agwaru, First Recipient of Heart Surgery

Ms. Grace Agwaru, first recipient to receive heart surgery through the GOL program, is a native of Uganda, and an agricultural economist who became the first recipient of the program sponsored and hosted to receive heart surgery at Saint Francis Hospital, Manhasset, Long Island, NY in 1974. Ms. Agwaru was four years old then.

This program, initiated by the Rotary Clubs of Manhasset, New York and Kampala, Uganda, provides heart surgery to children from countries where lifesaving surgical procedures are not available. Over its thirty-three-year existence, the Gift of Life Program, established in fifty-two countries, provided surgery to more than 10,000 children, and it was one of the favorite charities of former First Lady Nancy Reagan.

Ms. Agwaru gave a moving account of how grateful she was that Rotarians gave her the "Gift of Life." When she was four years old, she simply had a dream to be a child, but she soon learned she had a hole in her heart, and diagnosed not live to adulthood. As the first program recipient, and since so many had sacrificed for her, she was inspired to use her life to give back to others. Ms. Agwaru is currently a Community Development Manager at the Foundation for Education, Research, and Rural Development in the Teso region of Uganda. Funded by the Pearl of Africa Foundation, the organization in Teso is a nonprofit, nongovernmental foundation whose aim is to enhance the lives of the people of the Kumi District in Eastern Uganda. Uganda was given the name, "Pearl of Africa" by Winston Churchill when he was overcome by Uganda's magnificent natural beauty.

Ms. Agwaru is very active in microfinance, education, and other community programs. She has also started a Rotary Club in Uganda, which is working to provide open-heart surgery for more than 350 children in Uganda awaiting this medical procedure. She received a standing ovation by many when she told conference attendees, "When we save the life of one person, we are also saving the life of thousands of people, and by saving my life, you have helped me to reach out to the poor in my community."

Frank C. Collins Jr., Rotary Representative to the United Nations

Frank C. Collins Jr. hosted the very inspiring and informative Annual Rotary at the United Nations Day. There were more than 500 Rotarians in attendance, 200 Rotary Interact Club high school students, the President and President Elect of Rotary International, the Director of the Rotary International Foundation, Frank Devlyn, and many of Rotary International's directors and senior officers.

In his opening remarks, Mr. Collins spoke about how Rotary has been involved with the United Nations since its creation in1945. Over Forty-five of the founding delegates and up to seven Secretary-Generals were Rotarians. He clarified, however, that while Rotary participates in the humanitarian projects, we do not get involved in the political discussions of the UN.

Ankara, Turkey Conflict Resolution Conference Organized by Rotarians Kaan Soyak and Giorgio Balestrieri, Rotary Club of New York

April 2005

New York Rotarian and Co-chair of the International Division, Mr. Kaan Soyak, briefly discussed the Conflict Resolution Conference in Ankara that was held on March 18, 2005. Rotarians from the Yerevan and Gyumri Clubs in Armenia, the Tbilisi Club of Georgia, the Baku Club of Azerbaijan, and Rotarians from District 2430 in Turkey, District 5230 in California, as well as the Rotary Club of New York, attended this three-day conference.

Mr. Soyak pointed out that the participants successfully planned youth and cultural exchange programs and other activities to increase social, economic, and commercial relations between the four countries. "We were expecting fifty to sixty Rotarians to attend, but there were more than four hundred. Representatives of the foreign ministers from the respective four countries also participated in the "Caucasus Friendship Days."

Their next project is to establish a Rotary Club in Iraq. They have already started the preliminary exploration. "Rotary principles and the Four-Way Test are the best tools to bring Iraqi business people together regardless of what ethnic group," Mr. Soyak stated.

President Carl-Wilhelm Stenhammar of Rotary International

President Carl-Wilhelm Stenhammar of Rotary International provided additional insight and inspiration to our organization of business and professional men and women. He stated that he is proud to be Rotarian because we work for peace and better understanding of people. He happily announced that at that morning's Rotary International Board Meeting, new Rotary Clubs in the Peoples Republic of China and Cuba were now being established. "We will now have Rotary Clubs in 170 countries, and we hope that in the near future Rotary will have clubs in all the countries of the United Nations."

President Stenhammar shared his view that the best way for Rotary work for peace is through the youth programs of Rotary. He said, "If we could have every seventeen-year-old be an exchange student, we would have no more wars." He also noted that many poverty eradication programs are too big for any one organization to solve. Therefore, Rotary's "cooperation and continuity" through the World Health Organization and UNICEF to eradicate polio has proven to be very effective. He encouraged Rotarians to continue to concentrate their respective efforts on the MDGs (Millennium Development Goals), especially water and literacy projects. "Water is a gift of nature, and we cannot produce more; the water we drink today was here with the dinosaurs." He also asked Rotarians to encourage political leadership of the world to support the achievement of the United Nations MDGs.

Rotary International's "World Peace Fellowships"

RI (Rotary International) Alternate Representative to the United Nations, Sylvan Barnet, spoke about Rotary World Peace Fellows who are graduates of the Rotary Centers for International Studies in Peace and Conflict Resolution Program. These scholars will be a part of tomorrow's solution in promoting greater tolerance and cooperation among people worldwide. Rotary World Peace Fellows, who are chosen from a wide variety of countries, can help future leaders advance knowledge and understanding.

The Rotary World Peace Centers are located in eight leading universities around the world and selected scholars generally study at a master's level program in conflict resolution, peace studies, international relations, and other related disciplines.

The seven universities that have partnered with Rotary International are:

1. Duke University and University of North Carolina at Chapel Hill, North Carolina, USA
2. University of Bradford, West Yorkshire, England
3. University of Queensland, Brisbane, Queensland, Australia
4. International Christian University, Tokyo, Japan
5. Universidad del Salvador, Buenos Aires, Argentina
6. University of California, Berkeley, California, USA
7. Chulalongkorn University, Bangkok, Thailand

Each Rotary district may submit one candidate for competition in the worldwide selection process for up to 60 Rotary World Peace Fellowships offered annually. All Rotary Clubs are encouraged to recruit qualified candidates to apply for the Fellowship and to nominate a candidate for the competition. Rotary Foundation Scholarships for International Understanding are for one year of study in any country that has Rotary Clubs.

Temple Solar Project, Rotarian Paul M. Munson

Temple Solar Project Rotarian, Paul M. Munson represented District 6450 of Illinois and outlined the Temple Solar Project that donates solar ovens (that can bake, broil, and steam food) to developing countries. In Haiti, for example, it is estimated that women spend 55% of their income buying charcoal. As deforestation expands, wood and charcoal will become even more expensive.

The ovens are manufactured by Sun Ovens and were designed by a Milwaukee Rotarian. Ovens are mobile and easy to set up. By working with local Rotary Clubs, the Rotary Foundation may provide matching grants. Sun Ovens have been placed in China, North Korea, Afghanistan, Tsunami affected areas, and throughout Africa.

Hunger Plus, Inc. Project, J.B. Roberts, PDG (Past District Governor), R.C. of Plainview, Texas

Hunger Plus, Inc. Project, J.B. Roberts, PDG, R.C. of Plainview, Texas talked about the Hunger Plus, Inc. project where Rotarians collaborate with USAID (United States Agency for International Development) and USDA (United States Department of Agriculture) to send food, especially dehydrated products due to the long shelf life, around the world.

(For more information go to *http://www.hungerplus.org/*)

The Rotary Foundation, Frank Devlyn, Chairman

The Rotary Foundation Chairman, Frank Devlyn, stated that over the decades many Rotarians have helped others see by treating blindness in many ways. But, Rotarians also ask others to see in a different way. They ask people to see the suffering around them and see what they can do to help. Conversely, "the worst kind of blindness is for those who do not see the needs that exist all over the world." Rotarians need to give their four T's: Thinking, Talents, Time, and Treasure. Rotary is involved in every one of the MDGs in some way, and since we have over 106 fellowships, why not a fellowship for each Millennium Development Goal or a "Friends of the United Nations" Fellowship.

"Three Instruments to Foster Global Business Ethics" *By Josef Klee, PhD*

The Need for Global Business Ethics,
The Rotary Four-Way Test, the UN Global Compact,
& the Global Economic Ethic Manifesto

Dr. Klee is a former UN Deputy-Director and Advisor to the Holy See Mission to the UN. He has published four books and more than 60 articles about management topics. Presently, he is Adjunct Professor at the St, Thomas University in Miami.

The Need for Global Business Ethics

The latest global financial and economic crisis has intensified discussions about business ethics which have become a topic of widespread interest. Today, politicians, business leaders, clergy, scholars, etc. all participate in the debate about ethical issues related to the economy and the conduct of business operations.

Business ethics are not a new or recent matter of concern. Throughout history, there have always been merchants and business owners who, in their business dealings, have applied certain values or virtues and moral principles often rooted in their religious beliefs.

At the beginning of the last century, however, business leaders and scholars recognized the need for a common ethical framework for operating a business and began to address business ethics in a more systemic fashion.

Rotary International, founded in 1905, was among the first global organizations to adopt a set of ethical principles to be observed by its members with respect to their professional and business responsibilities. From the outset, practicing high ethical standards in business and professions is one of Rotary's guiding principles for its membership.

In the academic world, Catholic universities took the lead in establishing chairs for business ethics.

Since the Second World War and in particular after the corporate scandals in the 1980s, the interest in the issue of business ethics exploded; and most of the leading business schools invested heavily in business ethics programs.

Considering these efforts to promote and to teach business ethics, one must ask the question, how to explain the many scandals and serious ethical management offenses in recent years. Serious doubts remain whether one can successfully teach values, virtues, and good ethical behavior with the objective to ensure proper, just, and fair business operations.

This also raises the question concerning the wisdom of constructively teaching ethics in business schools. How can a graduate of a business school reconcile the dilemma to be expected to act as an aggressive and smart manager geared towards maximizing profits or shareholder value as taught in classes of marketing or finance, and at the same time, to practice social responsibility as taught in the ethics course?

Since the fall of the Soviet Empire, we have witnessed a rapid pace of economic globalization. Both political and business leaders have recognized that the world needs a new approach to dealing with the challenges of globalization, in particular, regarding its negative effects in developing countries as well as concerning the state of business in industrialized nations. There is a consensus in the international community that the global economy can only function effectively if it operates within a framework of ground rules for a fair and sustainable commercial exchange, and for cooperation. Such a framework must include ethical principles which are accepted in all cultures and traditions.

In my understanding, there are three important public examples of ethical principles, which enjoy universal acceptance and can serve as guidance for participants in the global economy.

These three instruments are:

1. The Rotary Four-Way Test
2. The United Nations Global Compact
3. The Global Economic Ethic Manifesto

These three instruments share similar values and ideals and pursue the same objective, namely to encourage and foster the application of high ethical standards in business. All three instruments rely on voluntary observance and are not legally binding. They serve as a moral/ethical code or guide for proper attitudes and behavior in conducting business decisions and operations.

At some level, these instruments are connected and complement each other. For example, Rotary International and the United Nations Global Compact Office have specifically recognized and acknowledged that they share the same values implied in their work. They have established a formal agreement of cooperation in a joint letter "to encourage a set of joint activities to advance the shared ideals of high ethical business practices, sustainable humanitarian action, and world peace and understanding."

In a similar way, the Global Economic Ethic Manifesto and the United Nations Global Compact are linked by mutual understanding and support. Both instruments share core values which are universally accepted; and Hans Kung, the initiator of the Manifesto, has expressly stated that the Manifesto intends to support the Global Compact from the angle of ethics.

The Rotary Four-Way Test

Rotary International, the world's first service club organization, is truly a universal and global organization. More than 1.2 million members live and serve in 200 countries. Rotary enjoys all over the world a unique reputation for its high ideals of service and its hands-on approach to assist people in need. The former United Nations Secretary-General, Kofi Annan, has described Rotary's highly successful signature program to eradicate polio "a shining example of private/public partnership."

From its inception, Rotary's mission, besides the ideal of service, included the obligation of its members to achieve high ethical standards in business and profession. Thus, as mentioned above, Rotary is considered as one of the pioneers in fostering business ethics.

In 1932, Herbert J. Taylor, a successful businessman and prominent Rotarian who also served as President of Rotary International, developed the Rotary Four-Way Test. In designing the test as an instrument to encourage and foster ethical behavior in business, Mr. Taylor had studied existing ethics codes and concluded that they were too long and difficult to memorize, rendering them impractical. His aim was to develop a simple guide in the form of a checklist because he believed one should not tell a person what he/she can or cannot do. Instead, a person should ask questions concerning his/her behavior, decisions, and actions in conducting business.

Finally, he formulated the so-called Four-Way Test consisting of four questions, which now constitutes the hallmark of Rotary International.

The four questions of the Test are:

1. Is it the Truth?
2. Is it Fair to All Concerned?
3. Will it Build Goodwill and Better Friendships?
4. Will it Be Beneficial to All Concerned?

Mr. Taylor and his managers themselves tested the new guide and applied it in their daily business dealings. With the application of the Four-Way Test, Mr. Taylor was able to make his company profitable and very successful.

In 1943, Rotary International officially adopted the Four-Way Test as an ethical guide for its members. The Test has been translated in more than one hundred languages, and in many Rotary Clubs worldwide, the Test is recited and reconfirmed regularly at the meetings.

In addition, many Rotary Clubs and Rotary Districts have developed special projects, such as essay and speech competitions regarding the meaning of the Test, as well as awards for outstanding applications of the Test to promote its dissemination.

The Rotary Four-Way Test as an instrument for business ethics has the distinctions that it is simple to apply and has proven its acceptance in all cultures; thus the Test has made a unique difference in the lives of Rotary members and the people they serve.

The United Nations Global Compact

The former United Nations Secretary-General, Kofi Annan, initiated the Global Compact. At the 1999 World Economic Forum in Davos, Switzerland, the Secretary-General had expressed his concern that the growing opposition to globalization in many parts of the world could impede free trade and free flow of investment, hinder sustainable economic growth, and ultimately threaten social, economic, and political stability worldwide.

He asked the business leaders not to wait for governments to impose new laws but to demonstrate responsibility and take the initiative for constructive change by embracing a set of nine principles for the practice of their global operations.

These principles are derived from universally accepted international agreements on human rights, labor standards, and environment protection, and they relate to the following issues.

In the area of human rights, business enterprises should:

- Support and respect the protection of human rights
- Ensure that they are not complicit in human rights abuses.
- Regarding labor standards, business enterprises should:
- Uphold the freedom of association and the right to collective bargaining
- Eliminate all forms of forced and compulsory labor
- Abolish child labor
- Eliminate discrimination in respect of employment and occupation
- Concerning the protection of the environment, business enterprises should:
- Support a precautionary approach to environmental challenges
- Undertake initiatives to promote greater environmental responsibility
- Encourage the development and the diffusion of environmentally friendly technology
- In 2004, a tenth principle, derived from the United Nations Convention against Corruption, was included in the Global Compact.
- This principle against corruption reads as follows:
- Business should work against corruption in all its forms, including extortion and bribery.

Companies wishing to engage in the Global Compact have to declare in writing to the United Nations Secretary-General that they support the principles of the Global Compact and are committed to take concrete actions such as:

- Issuance of a statement of support for the Global Compact addressed to the company's stakeholders, employees, customers, suppliers, and shareholders
- Application of the ten principles of the Global Compact in all corporate activities, submission to the Office of Global Compact of reports on concrete examples of progress made or lessons learned from implementing the principles
- Partnering with United Nations Organizations and NGOs (Nongovernmental Organizations) to assist in solving global problems

The Global Compact is a voluntary instrument. It is not a legally binding and enforceable code of conduct. Rather, the Global Compact is meant to foster constructive cooperation among the participants in dealing with the impact of globalization, and it is designed as a forum to share information and expertise for finding global solutions to remedy negative effects from globalization.

In July 2000, the Global Compact was formally launched at a meeting at the United Nations Headquarters in New York attended by about fifty leaders from business, labor, and civil society. Today, more than 7700 corporate participants and stakeholders from different industries and from every continent have joined the Global Compact.

Governments, trade associations, universities, and other institutions have organized events and meetings to present and to promote the Global Compact. Participating companies have organized national and regional networks to share their experience in applying the principles in their business strategies and operations. Also, companies cooperate with United Nations agencies and NGOs to provide humanitarian assistance or development aid in various parts of the world. In addition, universities have started to teach and conduct research on the Global Compact and related global issues.

However, the Global Compact has its critics. They claim that participating in the Global Compact allows companies to embellish their reputation, or that participating companies use the Global Compact for public relations purposes only without intending to ever change questionable corporate behavior.

In addition, some critics believe that the Global Compact is not effective because it functions on a voluntary basis, and therefore, lacks monitoring and enforcement authority.

The Global Compact is still evolving. Its success will ultimately be measured by how effectively its member corporations will cope with the challenges of globalization and how they will contribute to improving human rights, alleviating poverty, improving working conditions, protecting the environment, and eradicating corruption.

The Global Economic Ethic Manifesto

The Global Economic Ethic Manifesto was composed by a committee of German and Swiss scholars and senior business executives; and it was launched last year at the headquarters of the United Nations in New York in the presence of ambassadors and United Nations officials.

The Manifesto provides an ethical framework guiding the actions of the global economic and business community. In the words of Hans Kung: "It provides to everybody in these stormy seas an orientation as a chart to steer by, a map with clear ethical coordinates, … an ethical guideline for the difficult decisions that need to be taken in the harsh reality of everyday life."

The Manifesto is built on the values and principles expressed in the "Declaration toward a Global Ethic," issued by the Parliament of World Religions in 1993.

As indicated earlier, the Manifesto aims at supporting the United Nations Global Compact. Mr. Josef Wieland, one of the drafters of the Manifesto, states, "One of the intentions of the authors is for the Manifesto to provide individual and virtue-based ethical foundations to the management principles of the United Nations Global Compact."

The Manifesto is a rather elaborately worded document. Its text consists of a preamble and two chapters with thirteen articles. Its preamble outlines the vision, core values and principles of the Manifesto.

The first chapter defines the principle of humanity as "Being human must be the ethical yardstick of all economic action," and it consists of four articles.

Article 1: Economic action must fulfill human being's basic needs so that they can live in dignity.

Article 2: The dignity and self-esteem of all human beings are inviolable.

Article 3: To promote good and to avoid evil is the duty of all human beings.

Article 4: What you do not wish done to yourself do not do to others.

The second chapter defines different basic values of global economic activity and consists of nine more articles linked to four general headings.

Basic Values of Non-Violence and Respect for Human Life

Article 5: All human beings have the duty to respect the right to life and its development.

Article 6: Sustainable treatment of the natural environment is an uppermost value-norm for economic activity.

Basic Values of Justice and Solidarity

Article 7: Justice and the rule of law are fundamental values of economic life.

Article 8: The pursuit of profit is necessary for the survival of a business. The prevention of corruption is the duty of all stakeholders.

Article 9: Equal opportunity, distributive justice, and solidarity ensure sound economic development.

Basic Values of Honesty and Tolerance

Article 10: Truthfulness, honesty, and reliability are essential values to promote general human well-being.

Article 11: Diversity is a source of prosperity and discrimination of human beings violates the principles of ethics.

Basic Values of Mutual Esteem and Partnership

Article 12: Mutual respect, understanding, and fairness are indispensable for economic success.

Article 13: Partnership finds its expression in the ability to participate in economic life.

The authors of the Manifesto claim that its ethical principles, precepts, and stipulations are universal. It remains to be seen if the Manifesto will find worldwide acceptance. Due to its rather complex structure and particular stylistics concerning the wording of its text, the Manifesto is not an easy guide for daily use in corporations and government offices. However, the Manifesto is an excellent document to study and to teach global values and ethical principles both at universities and in the business world.

Conclusion

The three instruments discussed share the overall objective to foster ethical behavior in business and to provide principles and guidelines for achieving this goal. However, they differ widely concerning the focus and priority of specific targets of ethical behavior and of methods of implementation.

A company or organization interested in promoting ethics could choose one of the instruments, and if necessary, to make modifications to tailor it to its specific needs and corporate culture. It would be most important that the leadership of such a company or organization make a serious commitment to adoption and implementation, and do simply not pay lip-service for image and public relations purposes.

"The Plight of Religious Minorities in the Middle East" *By Josef Klee, PhD*

Advisor to the Holy See, Dr. Josef Klee gave a thoughtful analysis.

As we can hear and read in the media every day, the Middle East region is currently undergoing a historic and dramatic transformation in terms of political and constitutional structures. In this process, religious minorities such as Christians, Jews, and the Bahá'ís are severely restricted in practicing their religion, and often are persecuted under threat of physical harm, forcing them to leave their homelands.

The magazine *Newsweek* published, last month, an article about the persecution of Christians and concluded that terrorist attacks on

Christians in Africa, the Middle east, and Asia increased 309% from 2003-2010. The article states: "Christians are being killed in the Islamic world because of their religion. It is a rising genocide that ought to provoke global alarm."

We all know that the Middle East is the cradle of three world religions: Judaism, Christianity, and Islam; and that Christian minorities have co-existed in the Arab region for centuries. In spite of this historic fact, Christians in particular have been under attack and have been the object of escalating violence over the past several years.

As a consequence, the Arab world is being drained of its Christian residents; and the rate of Christian emigration from Lebanon, Jordan, Iraq, Egypt, Palestine, the Sudan, and Syria has reached unprecedented proportions. For instance, in the early 1990s, Iraq had approximately 1.5 million Christians out of a population of 18 million, then comprising more than 5% of the population. It is estimated that, at present, the Christian population is as low as 500,000. Christians in the Palestinian territories have dropped from 15% of the Arab population in 1950 to just 2% today. Both Bethlehem and Nazareth, which had been overwhelmingly Christian towns, now have strong Muslim majorities. Today, three-fourths of previously Bethlehem Christians live abroad, and more Christians from Jerusalem live in Sydney, Australia, than in their place of birth.

In Lebanon, Christians once constituted a solid majority of the country's population. Today, they number less than one million people and this number continues to shrink. In Egypt, Copts—the oldest religious community with about 11% of the population—have long felt the brunt of violent physical attacks from both the State radicals and Islamic fundamentalists. In the last months, the persecution of Copts has escalated.

In several other Islamic countries, conditions are fundamentally as worse. For example, in Nigeria, with the largest Christian minority (40 %), Muslims and Christians have lived on the edge of civil war, and Christians have suffered various forms of violence. Similarly, Christians in Sudan have been severely persecuted. In Saudi Arabia, Islam is the state religion and all citizens must constitutionally be Muslims. Accordingly, in Saudi Arabia, it is illegal to import, print, or own Christian or non-

Muslim religious materials.

Now, let's discuss what the outside world has done to alleviate the plight of religious minorities in the Middle East.

What has the United Nations done? Very early in 1948, the United Nations established the principle of protection of religious freedoms with the Universal Declaration of Human Rights. In general, the Universal Declaration of Human Rights proclaims in its Article 2 that "Everyone is entitled to all the rights and freedoms set forth in this Declaration, without distinctions of any kind, such as race, color, sex, language, religion, political or other opinion, national or social origin, property, birth, or other status." With its Article 18, the Universal Declaration of Human Rights stipulates in more detail, that "Everyone has the right to freedom of thought, conscience and religion; this right includes freedom to change religion or belief, and freedom, either alone or in community with others and in public or private, to manifest religion or belief in teaching, practice, worship, and observance."

Over the years, the United Nations has developed a number of additional human rights instruments and institutional mechanisms geared toward the promotion and observance of human rights protection worldwide, including the promotion of religious freedom, and protection from discrimination and persecution based on religion. In this respect, the United Nations Human Rights Body, in 1968, established the position of Special Rapporteur on freedom of religion or belief. The Special Rapporteur acts as an independent expert with the mandate to monitor and identify obstacles to the enjoyment of the right to freedom of religion or belief and to recommend ways and means to overcome the obstacles. He transmits letters of allegation and urgent appeals to states with regard to cases of infringements or impediments to the exercise of the right to freedom of religion or belief; he conducts fact-finding visits to countries in question; and he submits an annual report to the Human Rights Council and to the General Assembly on his activities and findings.

However, the effectiveness of the Special Rapporteur is rather limited since the office holder performs his/her functions only part-time, the funds for his/her office are very small, and many countries under review are not prepared to fully cooperate with the visits and appeals of the Special Rapporteur. In 2010, the General Assembly took another major step towards fighting persecution of religious minorities by adopting a very strongly worded resolution. This resolution condemns all forms of religious intolerance and discrimination as well as violations of freedom of religion or belief and emphasizes the obligation of states to investigate and punish acts of violence against persons belonging to religious minorities.

What has the United States done? The United States is perhaps the most active country in monitoring worldwide the status of religious freedoms and the occurrence of religious persecutions. The United States has established the USCIRF (United States Commission on International Religious Freedom), which is an independent, bipartisan US federal government commission. Its principal responsibilities are to monitor and review the facts and circumstances of violations of religious freedoms internationally, and to make policy recommendations to the President, the Secretary of State, and to the Congress. The work of this United States Commission on International Religious Freedom is based on international human rights standards, such as those established in the Universal Declaration of Human Rights and the International Covenant on Civil and Political Rights.

The Commission proposes countries to be closely monitored according to an established watch list, and it issues an annual report on the current situation regarding the protection of religious freedoms in those countries. It recommends which countries the Secretary of State should officially designate as "Countries of Particular Concern" because of engaging in or tolerating "systematic, ongoing, egregious violations of religious freedom." Once a country is designated a "Country of Particular Concern," the President is required by law to take action, including economic sanctions, or a decision to waiver of action. As of 2011, the Commission has recommended that the following 13 countries be designated as "Countries of Particular Concern": Burma, China, Eritrea, Iran, Iraq, Nigeria, North Korea, Pakistan, Saudi Arabia, Sudan, Turkmenistan, Uzbekistan, and Vietnam.

What have European countries done? The European Countries are also concerned with the issues of religious freedom and protection of religious minorities. Among the European countries, Italy is a very strong advocate for the protection of religious minorities. In 2011, the European

Parliament adopted a widely-backed resolution requesting sanctions against countries which do not protect religious minorities. Leaders from all political parties called for a review of current foreign policy instruments of the EU (European Union) to make them more suited to protecting Christian communities in third countries more effectively. The resolution lists proposed measures against states that knowingly fail to protect religious denominations. In particular, the EU stresses that silence and inaction are no options. However, the 27 Foreign Ministers were unable to adopt the resolution of the European Parliament because of political correctness. They could not agree in drafting their text that Christians were victims of religious persecution. Here I should mention that after the meeting, the "brave" Italian Foreign Minister expressed his disappointment and stated that the overemphasis of the prevailing secular culture would harm the credibility of Europe.

In 2010, after the initial attacks against Christian minorities in Iraq, Italy strongly supported an "EU Action Plan" which contains concrete measures to protect religious freedom in the world. The plan covers four areas, namely: bilateral actions, multilateral initiatives, financial support through the European Fund for Democracy and Human Rights, and training and capacity building. At the United Nations, Italy along with other EU partners, promotes each year at the General Assembly the previously mentioned UN resolution regarding the elimination of all forms of religious intolerance.

What has the Vatican done? The Holy See has been very vocal in defending religious freedom and condemning religious persecution. Since his election, Pope Benedict has often spoken out in defense of religious freedom and against persecution of Christians. In his message for the 2011 World Day of Peace, the Pope made a very strong case for religious freedom. In the introduction of his letter, the Holy Father referred to the killings of two priests and more than fifty worshipers in the Baghdad Cathedral and stated, "At present, Christians are the religious group which suffers most from the persecution on account of its faith." One of the Pope's suggestions is that all religious communities must defend the rights and freedoms of religious minorities. And the leaders of the great world religions and the leaders of nations should renew their commitment to promoting and protecting religious freedom, and in particular, religious minorities.

Also, this year in his New Year Address to the Ambassadors at the Vatican, the Pope strongly defended religious freedom and called for an end to the persecution of Christians. Pope Benedict has repeatedly expressed his concern regarding the precarious situation of Christians in the Middle East and has called for action against the persecution of Christians in this region. The pontiff has also repeatedly expressed his solidarity with the Copts and called on world leaders to protect them. In December of last year, at a meeting of the OSCE (Organization for Security and Cooperation in Europe), the "Foreign Minister" of the Vatican suggested that the OSCE should designate an annual international day against persecution and discrimination of Christians.

What have countries in the Middle East done? In general, the countries in the Middle East have shown very little interest and concern regarding the protection and promotion of religious freedom. Among the states in the Middle East, Jordan, a predominantly Muslim country, is a strong supporter of overall Christian-Muslim relations; and the members of the royal family have led the way in promoting interreligious dialogue. In an open letter launching the Common World initiative in 2007, Jordanian Prince Ghazi bin Muhammad bin Talal stated that all Jordanian citizens—Christians and Muslims—are equal citizens under Jordan's law and "all share in creating our country's future." During Pope Benedict's visit to Jordan in 2009, King Abdullah, in his address to the pope, stated that Muslims, Christians, and Jews—as "believers in the one God"—have an obligation to love God and to love one another, as uniform commandments found in the holy books of all three faiths. Furthermore, he emphasized the importance of dialogue to promote respect among believers and peace in the world.

Other voices in the Middle East exist who are advocates for religious freedom; but these are not strong enough to have an impact on the policy positions of their countries. What has the Civil Society done? One can find the strongest support for religious freedom and the protection of religious minorities in the civil society. In the last decade, dozens of NGOs (Nongovernmental Organizations) have been established to advocate on behalf of the protection of religious minorities. Many of these organizations are affiliated with religious denominations. Here, I can only mention a few examples which are not necessarily representative: The organization, "Aid to the Church in Need," with a seat in the UK monitors worldwide religious freedom issues and publishes a yearly report on the situation of religious minorities under the title: *A Report on Christians Oppressed for their Faith.*

Its 2011 edition covers more than 30 countries, providing pertinent statistics and describing in detail incidents of discrimination and violence against religious minorities.

Another active watchdog organization is the ICC (International Christian Concern) headquartered in Washington. This group has a strong advocacy function and provides practical support for persecuted Christian churches. It works through US government leaders (from US Congress, State Department, and the White House) to change legislation, bring pressure on persecuting countries, or to secure the release of the imprisoned Christians. It also provides practical help and financial assistance to persecuted communities and their underground pastors, as well as to the families of hunted, imprisoned, or murdered pastors. In addition, the Christian Concern group has a strong public awareness program through the distribution of reports and its daily news bulletins and press releases on religious violence, persecution, and discrimination. Also, the Christian Concern publishes an annual *Hall of Shame* list of countries that have the worst record regarding the persecution of Christian minorities. In 2011, this list contained eleven countries.

Coptic Solidarity is a newly founded NGO established to protect the human rights of Coptic communities, and to empower the Copts in Egypt so that they may attain full and inalienable citizenship rights and equality under Egypt's secular constitution and laws, in compliance with current international standards set by Human Rights conventions.

Specific activities of Coptic Solidarity include, among others: promoting political awareness and Human Rights Campaigns, lobbying for support at the international level, providing legal assistance in Egypt as needed to prosecute violations and criminals, and defending the religious rights of victims.

The Bahá'ís are a religious minority, which suffers grave persecution in various countries, especially in Iran. Hundreds of their members have been killed in Iran and thousands have been imprisoned. An organization named IPW (Iran Press Watch) closely monitors all incidents of persecution and discrimination against Bahá'ís, and it issues reports and press releases, which are widely distributed.

Finally, let me mention Pax Romana, which is an international Catholic student and professional organization. I am a member of Pax Romana and together with a few friends, we have established a tiny office in New York with the objective to advocate within the UN community the protection of religious minorities in the Middle East and raise awareness of the persecution of Christians in the Middle East. We meet with diplomats and UN staffers to lobby for our cause, we organize seminars and events at universities, conduct briefings for visiting students groups, and compile information on the topic.

Closing Remarks

So many initiatives exist, both at the international and at the local level, to promote religious freedom and to protect religious minorities. But so far, all these efforts have not shown real results. In the last year, the number of cases of violence particularly against Christians in the Middle East and also in the Far East, has increased.

We need a much stronger campaign at the international level to stop persecution and discrimination of religious minorities. Many countries are reluctant to address this issue in meetings at international organizations. In other words, the struggle will be a very difficult and long one. It is up to each and every one of us to participate in this great human rights cause. We can join and support advocate organizations. Personally, I wish Rotarians would get involved in this struggle and help to put an end to the persecution and suffering of religious minorities. In these unfortunate circumstances, silence and inaction are certainly no options.

The *Newsweek* article expresses this sentiment with the following conclusion: "The conspiracy of silence surrounding this violent expression of religious intolerance has to stop. Nothing less than the fate of Christianity, and ultimately of all religious minorities in the Islamic world, is at stake." Similarly, as Martin Luther King stated, "In the end, we will remember not the words of our enemies but the silence of our friends."

"Peacemaking in Action: The Case for Nepal," Mikio Tajima, Rotary Club of New York, *(this article written by Sheila Washington)*

Eight-thirty in the morning, February 21, 2007, on a beautiful NY morning, the meeting of the Rotary Club of NY at the UN was called to order by Dr. Nikolaus Helbich. Three interns from Germany were among the visitors. After introduction of guests and a sumptuous breakfast catered by the Penthouse Café at the German Mission, Director Giorgio Balestrieri introduced the speaker, Dr. Mikio Tajima.

Dr. Tajima, a New York Rotarian, is a UN Director Retiree, Professor Emeritus Kawansei Gakuin University, Japan, and UN Global Compact Advisor. In 1972 he visited Nepal as a member of a UN Fact-finding Mission to South Asian landlocked countries. What he witnessed at Biratnagar, the major transit point with India and Nepal, made him an instant sympathizer and supporter of Nepal. Upon retirement from the UN he formed RC21 (Reconciliation 21), a conflict prevention NGO with a mission to strengthen Nepal's NGO system, and coordinate outside efforts to bring productivity and stability to the country.

Nepal is a Kingdom of about 27 million people, mostly Hindus. Its monarchy ruled for nearly 240 years until 1990 when there was the first people's uprising. At that time the King agreed to install a multiparty system. Subsequently, elections were held and a Parliament was installed. In 1995 the head of the CPN (Communist Party of Nepal), which was then the majority party, became the Prime Minister. In short order, he was dismissed resulting in the party splitting into two groups the CPN/M (Maoist) and the CPN/UML (Unified Marxist-Lenin). Both groups opposed the monarchy. The former resorted to force while the latter denounced the use of force and remained the legitimate political party.

In February 2005, the fifteen-year democratic exercise came to an end. The King, Gyanendra Bir Bikram Shah Dev dismissed Prime Minister Deuba and his government, declared himself an absolute monarch and took direct control of the army. Massive arrests, suspension of civil liberties, and declaration of a state of emergency followed. Communication with the outside world was cut as a stunned international community looked on. The King's undemocratic actions resulted in the seven large political parties forming SPA (Seven Party Alliance), an alliance with commitments and closer ties with the Maoists.

With the widespread political discontent the SPA and the Maoists began a program of nationwide strikes and mass street protests. After 19 days and with the decisive support of civil society groups, the King handed over power to the political parties and reinstated Parliament. On April 28, 2006, Parliament convened and a new Prime Minister, Girija Prasad Koirala, commonly known as G. P. Koirala, was sworn in two days later.

The King's army was renamed the "National Army" and placed under Prime Minister Koirala's control. Under increasing pressure from the international community, the UN was allowed to open the OHCHR (Office of the United Nations High Commissioner of Human Rights). With this action, the UN began to emerge as a positive outside force in the eyes of the people of Nepal.

The SPA and the Maoists signed a ceasefire agreement and decided to hold Constituent Assembly elections in June 2007. The biggest challenge for the new government was the disarming of the Maoists insurgents. However, both the SPA and the Maoists agreed to entrust the arms management task to the UN. In addition, Nepal's list of pressing issues also includes a new constitution, the King's future, and the shape of the new national government (federal or another model).

Dr. Tajima underscored the point that the peace process alone will not be sufficient nor be sustainable unless accompanied by confidence-building measures at various levels of its civil society. He travels to Nepal in early March for a two-day roundtable with university students, teachers, businessmen, political leaders, and mass media in Kathmandu, the capital. The theme of the meeting is promotion of a peace culture (tolerance, reconciliation and forgiveness). The objectives are to begin the reconciliation organizing and create implementation plans to enable the mobilization of networking support.

In conclusion, Dr. Tajima expressed his hope that the resulting guidelines and "think pieces" from this and subsequent meetings will be used by international NGOs, university students, and others to promote awareness around the world regarding Nepal.

When the meeting adjourned at 9:45, it was clear that the people of Nepal have a dedicated and highly motivated champion in Dr. Tajima.

Postscript:

As if to confirm Dr. Tajima's mission, on March 4, 2007, *The New York Times* published an article about traveling in Nepal, headlined, "As Political Unrest Eases, Travel Picks Up." The article cited developments such as, the signed peace deal with the Maoist rebels after 10 years of bitter conflict, the temporary constitution now in effect, and the interim Parliament that is bringing stability to the country. The UN Security Council voted in January to set up a mission to oversee the disarmament and cease-fire accord. This adds to reasons being cited for the renewed interest and the return of adventure-oriented travelers to Nepal.

Guatemala Literacy Project, Rotarian Glenn Chamberlain, Ephrata, Washington.

Glenn retired from local city politics in 1990 and has since made 9 trips to Guatemala to enhance literacy by providing books to impoverished schools. Under this model, a Rotary Club provides the initial books and the children's families pay a small fee for the books. The initial books should last for five years and the fee that was paid by the students is used to purchase replacements.

President of Rotary International, Dong Kurn Lee, and the Chairman of the Bubang Manufacturing Company in Seoul, Korea.

He joined Rotary in 1971, and in 1996 he chartered thirty-two new clubs and added 1,800 new Rotarians to his district.

It was only two months earlier, when President Dong Kurn Lee, known as D.K., addressed government and civic leaders at the forum convened by UN Secretary-General Ban Ki-Moon on September 25, 2008. At the forum attended by top government and civic leaders, President D.K. reaffirmed Rotary's commitment to working with the UN to eradicate polio, and to build a healthier, more peaceful world. He stated, "Rotary has helped to bring the world closer to the end of a disease, and to the achievement of the fourth Millennium Development Goal of reducing child mortality." In a speech during a breakout session on health and education, President D.K. said, "We have created partnerships that will endure and will yield benefits far beyond the elimination of one disease."

At today's address to Rotarians, President D.K. confirmed that Rotary is a very diverse organization, but we know that on the inside, people are all alike, and we trust in the same "golden rule." When a country or village needs assistance, Rotarians do not consider how the people dress, how they speak, or how they pray. He said, "What matters is that they are all human beings and they need help." As a result, for the last twenty years we have partnered with the United Nations. Rotarians have donated $720 million to Polio eradication, have immunized more than 2 billion children in 122 countries, and we and our partners reduced polio cases by 99% in our organized PolioPlus Program. President D.K. concluded his address encouraging all of the 1.2 million Rotarians, in more than 200 hundred countries, to continue working to "Make Dreams a Reality."

"MDGs progress has been made in the aggregate, but not in all countries."

Rotary Books for the World Program, Charles Clemmons, PDG, R.C. of Seabrook, Texas

Rotarian Charles Clemmons and his wife, Barbara, are recipients of the Rotary International's Service Above Self Award. With vast Rotary service, Charles and Barbara Clemmons co-founded the "Books for the World Project," which collects used books from schools, libraries, and individuals and then ships them to Southern and Eastern Africa. The program has sent over eighty shipping containers of books over the last few years. Many of the used books are collected from school districts in Texas and then sent to Johannesburg, South Africa. The Texas and African school districts are storing the containers, and students are stacking and distributing the books.

The containers' sea transport cost about $4,100, and a container itself cost about $2,100 to purchase. Stemming from a recent promotion, Johannesburg Rotarians have received more than 7,000 requests for books. Mr. Clemmons also underscored the might of Rotary International Foundation's Matching Grants to leverage the funding. The program, however, does not ship to countries that require custom duties to be paid on the books.

President of Rotary International, John Kenny, R.C. of Grangemouth, Scotland

President of Rotary International, John Kenny of the R.C. of Grangemouth, Scotland has been a Rotarian since 1970, and is a past dean of his local law faculty, and a judge. He is a major donor to Rotary Foundation, and has received the Foundation's Meritorious Service and Distinguished Service Awards.

President-elect Kenny gave a brief, yet insightful address insuring that our real riches are those that we keep inside us, commonly known as our values. Those of us that have joined Rotary, know it is not only our thoughts, but our actions that make a difference. Rotarians take actions to intelligently prevent war and to end the reasons for it. We train future leaders, conduct international service projects addressing water, health, hunger, and education by establishing international fellowships with emphasis on ethical and honest behavior, with the other Rotarians in more than two hundred countries and geographic regions. The incoming president concluded that we want to bring solutions to the problems of the world, and Rotary is the organization that helps us to do this.

International Diabetes Federation: Dr. Martin Silink, R.C. of Lane Cove, Australia

Dr. Martin Silink, R.C. of Lane Cove, Australia, is a professor of Pediatric Endocrinology at the University of Sydney. He is also President of the International Diabetes Federation: the umbrella group of over 200 diabetes associations in more than 160 countries.

Dr. Silink gave encouragement and thanks to New York Rotarian and Rotary International representative to the UN, Mr. Sylvan Barnet. He thanked "Barney" for his "indispensable help to open the door and assist in the campaign for the UN resolution in 2006." The 2006 resolution recognized that diabetes is a serious risk to family and the entire world, and designated Friday, November 14, 2008 as .World Diabetes Day.

Dr. Silink pointed out that diabetes in the developing world it is an epidemic. Two hundred fifty million people worldwide or six percent of adults have diabetes, and it is increasing by seven million individuals each year.

There are two types of diabetes. Type 1 is due to insulin deficiency, and Type 2 is primarily caused by obesity and insulin resistance. Approximately 440,000 children have Type 1 diabetes and 70,000 are in truly desperate circumstances. Due to lack of access to insulin, for example, the life expectancy of children with diabetes in Mozambique and Malawi is less than one year.

The doctor pointed out than several Rotary Clubs in Australia have partnered and have supplied insulin and syringes for 1,000 children in eighteen countries. He also pointed out that the cost of insulin is prohibitive in many countries. The average number of days one would need to work to buy one month of insulin is more than two weeks salary in many countries.

Pink Piggy Banks, Wayne Edwards, PDG, R.C. of Tallahassee, Florida

Mr. Wayne Edwards, PDG, R.C. of Tallahassee, Florida, a certified Financial Planner, outlined his district's efforts to assist in the fight against diabetes. Mr. Edwards underscored that there is no vaccine for diabetes, and without insulin a diabetic child will die. With this in mind, each Rotary Club in the Tallahassee Rotary district was given "Pink Piggy Banks" donated by Walgreens Drug Stores, and each club was asked to make a donation.

The clubs raised $25,000, leveraged this initial amount with District Designated Funds and a Rotary International Matching Grant, and the $25,000 grew to $106,000 dollars. Using this funding in partnership with the International Diabetes Foundation, the Tallahassee Club organized a diabetes camp in Bolivia. Seven Bolivian clinics were established to instruct diabetic children on how to live with diabetes, provide the insulin they needed, and arrange transportation for parents and the patients to the clinics. Since then, the Bolivia Program has now expanded and established several clinics in Nigeria and Cameroon.

In addition, Eli Lilly and Company's Lilly Foundation donated $180,000 placed in trust with the Rotary Foundation for the project. The corporation also produced a video about the program that has been nominated for an Academy Award. Rotarian Edwards was informed at today's conference that an Insulin Rotary Action Group has been approved by the Rotary International Board of Directors at their preconference meeting.

Seed Programs Inc., John Batcha, R.C. of North Mecklenburg County, North Carolina

Mr. John Batcha, R.C. of North Mecklenburg County, North Carolina was an Executive Director of the Asgrow Seed Company that distributes garden seeds to twenty-nine countries. He is now President of Seed Programs, Inc. and partners with Rotarians "Sowing Seed to Fight World Hunger."

This program is based on the ancient proverb: *If you give a man a fish, you feed him for a day; if you teach him to fish, you feed him for life.* Mr. Batcha emphasized that the Rotary Seed Program does not give food; it teaches children how to grow their own food.

It also provides informational material to plant the seeds and partners with Peace Corps volunteers to work with schools and orphanages to plant local gardens in developing countries. Seed Programs International has already sent eleven million packages that planted one million gardens in sixty countries. The vegetables produced are rich.

RI (Rotary International) President Elect, Wilfred J. Wilkinson, R.C. of Trenton, Ontario, Canada

Rotary International President-elect, Wilfred J. Wilkinson, R.C. of Trenton, Ontario, Canada addressed the conference and added that for true peace, there must be a healthy and educated population. Whenever Rotarians are faced with problems too large to even contemplate, they start small and keep on going. The President-elect also noted that Rotary builds bridges of friendships, and while the bridges may be small they may last for hundreds of years. But most importantly, Rotarians have built thousands and thousands of these bridges. He concluded his remarks with "We may never live in a world of total peace, but we as Rotarians know that we have helped achieve peace, and let today's meeting encourage us to do even more."

RI Foundation Chairman, Luis Vicente Giay, R.C. of Arrecifes, Argentina

RI Foundation Chairman, Luis Vicente Giay, R.C. of Arrecifes, Argentina humorously stated that he only was only allocated five minutes to speak about the great success of the Rotary Foundation, however, in most South America countries five minutes is not even enough time to say hello. Nevertheless, Chairman Luis provided stirring insight into our Foundation. He informed Rotarians that larger donations are increasing to the Rotary Foundation because of the credibility of Rotary. Donors know that Rotary funds go straight to the project and not for more fund-raising or high salaries. He concluded by assuring Rotarians that it is our Foundation that also makes us proud to be Rotarians.

Socially Conscious Coffee, Martin Postma, R.C. of Westminster, Colorado

Martin Postma, R.C. of Westminster, Colorado spoke about the Socially Conscious Coffee project that is providing for the first time, education, healthcare, and economic opportunity to the coffee bean growers of Northern Brazil. This program is also providing vocational skills training, and is purchasing products from regional businesses to help develop the local economy. Known in Portuguese as the Centro Rural Educafe, children from the Sinay Neves coffee farms and several neighboring coffee farms are now receiving a quality education and regular meals. In addition, local adult coffee farm workers and their wives also have the opportunity to learn how to read and write.

Ethiopian Water Project, Rotarians David Spicer and Ezra Teshome, R.C. University District, Seattle, Washington

Ethiopian Water Project, Rotarians David Spicer and Ezra Teshome, R.C. University District, Seattle, Washington, spoke about their partnership with four countries and four districts in the Ethiopian Water Project. This project trains local villagers to keep water wells clean, operational and sustainable. Very often water wells last only a few years after construction from overuse, lack of maintenance, and accountability. This program builds water wells, provides training, and encourages responsible villagers to charge a small fee to finance the maintenance and supervision of the wells to insure sustainability.

The Rotary Clubs in Addis Ababa in Ethiopian (District 9200) help provide funding and coordinate with the Seattle Rotary Clubs and "Water Partners" in prioritizing the most critical areas of need. They also provide oversight of the water projects and financial accountability.

Safe Blood for Africa, Warren Kaufman, R.C. of Carmel Valley, California

Mr. Warren Kaufman, R.C. of Carmel Valley, California, outlined his club's Safe Blood Africa Program. While he was a Rotary Group Study Exchange Team Leader in Nigeria, Mr. Kaufman noticed many unnecessary deaths due to unsafe blood transfusions. Too often when a Nigerian needed an emergency transfusion, a family member was forced to purchase a pint or two from someone who was not healthy, primarily from lack of food or alcohol use. The blood was then transferred "hot" without the benefit of disease testing—HIV/AIDS positive or blood typing. When a person receives a transfusion from an AIDS infected donor, the patient will 100% of the time contract HIV/AIDS or hepatitis as well as most other blood-borne diseases.

The Safe Blood Africa Program sends refrigerated blood banks with a generator and training material for safe blood handling to sites selected by Nigerian Rotary Clubs.

The cost for the blood bank package is about $20,000. However, the Rotary system of matching grants makes participation in the program affordable for most clubs. Each blood bank is funded through a partnership that includes one or more clubs in District 6780 in California, a Nigerian club in District 9120, and the Rotary Foundation. For example, the donor club raised $6,000. The district governor can then contribute $6,000 in the DDF (District Designated Fund), the district portion of Rotary Foundation contributions, and District 9120 in Nigeria contributed $100 in the DDF. This total is then matched by the Rotary Foundation in the amount of $12,100, with $24,200 now available.

In 2005 the Safe Blood Africa Program sent four blood banks to Nigeria and twenty more blood banks are planned for this year. It is estimated that 11,000 lives have already been saved in Africa by the project.

The Rotarian Magazine, Janice Chambers, Senior Editor

The Rotarian Magazine, Ms. Janice Chambers, Senior Editor, gave a very insightful presentation on the Crisis in Niger where she visited and then wrote the cover page article in the September, 2005 Rotarian. She pointed out that Niger, very often confused with Nigeria, is one of the 14 African countries in Rotary District 9100 and has the dubious distinction of being the world's poorest nation. The average birth rate is also among the highest with 8 births per-woman and a life expectancy of only 44 years. Each year, it suffers from cyclical famine when all the grain has been consumed before the new harvest. As a result, the country slides even further into poverty. In September 2005, nearly a third of the country's 12 million people faced starvation. UNICEF officials report that the situation is still critical.

Rotary International Receives Award From The United Nations Association

The President of Rotary International, Mr. Wilfred Wilkinson, gave an inspiring examination of how, with the efforts of Rotary, Peace is Possible. President Wilfred had been in New York on October 25, 2007 to accept an award on RI's behalf from the United Nations Association of New York in recognition of Rotary's contribution in providing access to clean water to villages around the world and its work on the global water crisis.

He emphasized that if we are to teach real peace in the world, and if we are to carry on a real war against war, we will have to start with the children. Anger and hatred are not inherited, they are learned, and children who see hate, learn hate. But people in conflict can achieve peace, and Rotarians can help because "Rotary is a long-standing, nonreligious, nonpolitical organization, and we are not beholden to any prime minister or government," he noted.

He also wanted his fellow Rotarians to keep in mind that a "person becomes great to the degree for which he works for his fellow man." Each of us has the opportunity to build peace and create bridges by collaborating with the United Nations to achieve the Millennium Development Goals.

"Building bridges, even small ones, is something that many Rotarians have done very well," he added.

He noted that this year Rotarians and guests from dozens of countries gathered recently for three Rotary Presidential Peace Forums.

They were:

- Boyana, Bulgaria, in August, 2007 that invited participants to discuss the possibilities of peace with a focus on the Balkans
- Istanbul, Turkey on September 1, 2007 which coincided with the UN World Peace Day initiative with a focus on peace in the Middle East
- Nairobi, Kenya, on September 20, 2007 that outlined Rotary's role in building peace in Africa

Casa Amparo ala Mujer (House of Mercy for Women), Barbara Walters, R.C. of Kalamazoo, Michigan

Mrs. Barbara Walters, R.C. of Kalamazoo, Michigan is a reporter and columnist with the *Kalamazoo Gazette* and she first became involved in Rotary when she was assigned by her newspaper to report on a Rotary eleven-day Caravan drive to Belize. Mrs. Walters arranged for her club to provide a full-time certified teacher for Casa Amparo ala Mujer that served as a shelter for abandoned girls in Reynosa, Mexico, which is across the border from Texas. The shelter is managed by Catholic nuns who provide for the physical, spiritual, emotional, and educational needs of these children who have nowhere to turn. Today, the shelter serves close to one hundred girls from ages six to seventeen.

Mrs. Walters recognized that many of the girls needed additional assistance to learn to read and write. Poor reading and writing skills made employment opportunities difficult for these girls when they entered adulthood and could send them back into the cycle of poverty. In response to this in the mid-1990s, with used desks from public schools, the Rotary Club of Kalamazoo provided funding for a full-time, certified teacher for the home. In 1993, there were no children from the orphanage that entered high school and now, with the hired teacher, there have already been two girls that graduated from college. Recognizing success, the club is now funding a second teacher. Mrs. Walters also pointed out that 35 years ago she and her husband served as teachers for three years in Malawi. Hearing about her participation at this conference, one of Ms. Walter's former students, Steven Mackenzie, now the Ambassador to the United Nations for Malawi, arranged to meet with Mrs. Walters and her husband during her visit to New York. Insightfully, she noted that at times, teachers may forget some of their students, but seldom do students forget their teachers.

Rainwater Harvesting Program, John Boot, R.C. of Summerland, British Columbia, Canada

Rainwater Harvesting Program, Mr. John Boot, R.C. of Summerland, British Columbia, Canada outlined the Nakuru (Kenya) Rainwater Harvesting Program, a proven model for gathering rainwater into a tank that costs about $400 and lasts for 30 years. Nakuru is the provincial capital of Kenya's Rift Valley province, with roughly 300,000 inhabitants, and currently the fourth largest urban center in Kenya. He emphasized that given Rotary's incredible reach of 32,000 clubs in 172 countries, many tanks can be built. There is a need for 3,500 tanks to be built in the Nakuru area of Kenya alone. The tanks are financed by a combination of club-level fund-raisers, RI matching grants, and Canadian government matching grants. The families that receive the tank are required to pay fifty dollars, or contribute labor to help build other tanks in the community. The program has built over 1,200 tanks.

John outlined a number of points to remember when building these tanks:

- Search for new partners with sponsoring African clubs.
- Talk to the people involved.
- Let the recipients of the tanks do most of the work.
- Appropriate scale is vital—small projects work best.
- Plant 100 trees around the tank.

RI President-elect Dong Kurn Lee, from Seoul, Korea

RI President-elect Dong Kurn Lee, from Seoul, Korea is president of Yonsei Company, Ltd. and Bubang Techron Co. and has been a Rotarian since 1971.

He pointed out that the United Nations and other NGOs had a significant effect on the restoration of Korea when it was devastated by its civil war in the 1950s. The United Nations responded to the bleak situation by providing humanitarian aid. As a result, Korea was able to rise from the ruins of war and is now ranked third in Rotary Foundation contributions and fourth in Rotary membership. "That is because Korean Rotarians as well as all Rotarians believe that there a time to help, and a time to act," President-elect Lee noted.

Robert Scott, Chairman of The Rotary Foundation, R.C. Cobourg, Ontario

Mr. Robert Scott, Chairman of The Rotary Foundation, R.C. Cobourg, Ontario was born in Scotland, and is a graduate of Edinburgh University School of Medicine. Mr. Scott reaffirmed that the mission of The Rotary Foundation is to enable Rotarians to advance world understanding, goodwill, and peace through the improvement of health, the support of education, and the alleviation of poverty. It is supported solely by voluntary contributions from Rotarians and friends of the Foundation who share its vision of a better world.

The foundation supports thousands of water, health, and hunger programs, and they will bring about peace, but the world also needs peacemakers. He recommends that Rotarians also focus on the "Rotary Peacemakers" network, the thousands of Ambassadorial Scholars, Peace and Conflict Scholars, and Rotary World Peace Fellows that our foundation has sponsored, and the six Rotary Centers in partnership with seven leading universities.

Development of Treatment for Pediatric HIV/AIDS, Rotarian Dr. Stephen Nichols, Rotary Club of Yonkers, N.Y.

Dr. Stephen Nicholas, R.C. Yonkers, New York, is Professor of Clinical Pediatrics and Clinical Population and Family Health at Columbia University and has pioneered care for children and families with HIV/AIDS since 1983. Dr. Nicholas narrated a very encouraging presentation regarding the treatment and spread of pediatric HIV/AIDS. He has also directed clinical research in the Dominican Republic, Haiti, South Africa, and St. Petersburg, Russia.

While forty million people have HIV/AIDS and four million people still get it every year, tragically three million will die this year, it is a serious and grave crisis. However, Dr. Nicholas clearly noted that there is progress and hope for the eradication of global pediatrics HIV/AIDS (mother-to-child) and he described the major advances in HIV/AIDS treatment.

Back in the 1980s, the fight against HIV/AIDS seemed to be hopeless when infected children rarely lived beyond three years old even in the developed countries. However, doctors soon learned that mothers only occasionally transmitted HIV/AIDS to their children in utero. Most HIV/AIDS is spread the day of birth and by breastfeeding. As such, the first step in fighting global pediatric HIV/AIDS was to instruct, and make it possible for AIDs infected mothers not to breastfeed their babies, and to only have caesarian delivery.

A second major development in fighting AIDs was in 1989 when a new medication changed HIV/AIDS from being lethal, and then in 1996 the "AIDs Cocktail" was developed, and this significantly helped in the treatment. As a result, the treatment of AIDs infected mothers has been refined and has virtually stopped HIV from being passed to the child and this significantly stopped pediatric HIV in the United States and Europe.

However, in the developing countries, "hopelessness, and not funding," is the cause for the lack of political will to eradicate pediatric HIV transmission. Forty percent of infants will get HIV/AIDS if their mothers do not stop breastfeeding. However, if we treat the HIV infected mother and use bottle-feeding formula rather than breastfeeding, the rate of pediatric HIV is zero percent! Needless to say, the mothers need to be treated or all the babies saved will become AIDS orphans.

In the mid-1990s it cost about $10,000 for the drugs to treat this infection. Happily, in 2004, infected parents can be treated for about $300 year. In addition, drugs are usually available free of charge in many countries from the Global Fund for AIDs, Tuberculosis, and Malaria. Dr. Nicholas outlined the Rotary World Community Service Project in La Romana, Dominican Republic to prevent mother-to child HIV transmission and to reduce the number of orphans. The Dominican Republic and Haiti have the highest rate of AID's outside of Sub-Sahara Africa. This Family Aids Center was created by the RI Foundation and is supported by many local Rotary Clubs in New York.

RI Peace and Conflict Studies, Mr. Richelieu Marcel Allison

RI Peace and Conflict Studies, Mr. Richelieu Marcel Allison expressed his gratitude to The Rotary Foundation because it is recognized around the world as a "bringer of hope." He outlined how Liberia, founded by freed American slaves, which named its capital Monrovia after President Monroe, was engulfed in a brutal civil war in the early 1990s. As a young boy then, Mr. Allison witnessed firsthand the devastating effects of civil war and a countless number of dead bodies. Also, he expressed how frightening it was to know that you and your family could be killed by anyone with a gun.

Thankfully, Liberia has come a long way since then and is now an exemplary democracy actively rebuilding its civil society infrastructure. In 2006 Mr. Allison was selected to attend the Rotary International Peace and Conflict Studies program at Chulalongkorn University in Thailand. He was initially denied a visa, but the Ambassador was an alumnus of Chulalongkorn University and a visa was ultimately granted. Mr. Allison studied a three-month intensive program.

The program reinforced a "culture of peace" to be brought to West Africa including Liberia, Guinea, and Sierra Leone. Mr. Allison hopes to start a "Peace Caravan" in West Africa. Together these countries share border areas and local people can discuss peaceful solutions for their differences. "Everywhere there are conflicts, and therefore we need to invest in peace, and to invest in more peace-ambassadors for a better peace." Mr. Allison also said that he wished every individual could inculcate the "Four-Way Test" into all their actions to make a better world. He concluded his talk by quoting Martin Luther King, "We make peace by talking not to our friends, but by talking to our enemies."

Malaria Action Group, Brian Stoyel, Past President of Rotary: Britain and Ireland

Malaria Action Group, Mr. Brian Stoyel, Past President of Rotary, Britain and Ireland, received the Service Above Self Award in 1999. In 2003, he started Rotarians Eliminating Malaria in Tanzania and is chairman of Rotarians Eliminating Malaria Action Group. Mr. Stovel pointed out that this Rotary action group raises funds to provide ITNs (Insecticide Treated Nets), insecticides, and medicines as well as Haemocoel machines to monitor individuals for malaria. Funding is also provided for education and awareness programs by training local workers to go into villages to educate the local people to recognize symptoms, provide treatments, and take steps for prevention.

The project is based on getting the local clubs to take responsibility for the project and then supplying the technical expertise and equipment required. The two Rotary Clubs of Arusha, Tanzania are local partners for this program. Brian pointed out that one insecticide treated net costs less than $5.00, and four people can sleep under it. The recipients are asked to pay 1,000 Tanzanian shillings or about $1.50. The nets have the Rotary logo and are manufactured locally to save shipping costs and help the local economy. The nets have to be retreated every twelve months, but even if not treated the bed nets are still effective, but the mosquitoes are not destroyed.

Transylvania, Romania Dairy Program, Mr. Gary Parrish, R.C. of Little Rock, Arkansas

Mr. Gary Parrish, Past President of the R.C. of Little Rock, Arkansas, and a second generation Rotarian, outlined to the participants the "Farmers Feed the Children Program."

Mr. Parrish visited farming families in Romania where he noticed that many children had no energy because of lack of nutrients in their diet, and many families were impoverished. To help with this, his Club partnered with Heifer International, a nonprofit, charitable organization that is based in Little Rock, Arkansas and dedicated to relieving global hunger and poverty. It donates livestock and plants, and provides education in sustainable agriculture to financially disadvantaged families around the world. The animals are chosen to be large milk producers and appropriate for the Romanian farms.

In partnership with Heifer International, Mr. Parrish sketched out how the Rotary Club of Little Rock delivered two dairy cows to a farming family in the Transylvania area of Romania. In three months, the two heifers became four. Under this program, the first calf is donated back to another farmer, and 600 liters of milk per year are given to community centers such as schools and hospitals. The farmer can then sell the remaining milk on the open market.

When several months passed, he noticed that he saw once-poor farmers were now feeding poor children of other farmers. He also noticed that children were happier and healthier looking, and repairs were completed around their houses. Previously there was little protein in their diet, but thanks to this program, 20,000 children have benefited from a better diet.

A very important aspect of this program, Mr. Parrish pointed out, is that it is a hand-up, not a handout, and it is sustainable. He emphasized that Rotary also brought credibility, as well as providing a 3H grant to the project in view of the fact that Heifer International needed outside partners to keep this program going. The end result is that once again we have seen Rotary change lives, and we have built better friendships and goodwill, Mr. Parrish clearly illustrated.

After Mr. Parrish's presentation, Mr. William H. Luers, President of the United Nations Association, and former president of the Metropolitan Museum of Art explained that reform of the United Nations is needed because it is a different world than when the UN was created. There no longer is much danger of large countries going to war in the scale as when the UN was created. Now, the world has to deal with other issues for which no nation can defend itself, such as natural disasters and terrorism. "The world is different and the UN has to be different."

Regarding the "Oil-for-Food Programme" scandal, the investigation cost $30 million to essentially uncover that one individual may have stolen $130,000. Paul Volker's reports did, however provide suggestions for organizational direction, and management and transparency reform.

The UN agenda of the developed world is security oriented and the UN agenda of the developing countries is poverty reduction. The MDGs were a compromise to each group. It should be pointed out that the United States delegation at the UN was originally not in support of the MDGs, but after months of negotiation and refinement, the President of the United States announced his support at the UN Summit.

Several of the important points at the recent Summit are:

- Not able to define terrorism
- Security Council was not reformed
- Peacebuilding Commission has been designed to help build nations after conflict
- Human Rights Council to replace the degraded Human Rights Commission
- Responsibility of the UN to protect peoples from genocide

The Ambassador recommends that all Rotarians voice support to their elected officials for building a new United Nations relevant to the modern world.

Our Dear Friend, Sylvan "Barney" Barnet, Rotary International's Representative to the United Nations, Died on January 7, 2015

- Sylvan "Barney" Barnet's career spanned a productive seventy years.
- Rotary International and the Rotary Club of New York gave him the Rotary Award of Honor—the highest award for outstanding lifetime service.
- He received his BA from Yale in 1940.
- He served as a reserve officer in The United States Navy throughout WWII, saw action in both the Atlantic and South Pacific, and he retired from the Navy as a Lt. Commander.
- In 1954, Barnet became the General Manager of the European Edition of The New York Herald Tribune in Paris.

- In 1965, he joined the Department of Commerce as Deputy Director of the US Travel Service to promote both international tourism and business development in the United States.
- In 1968, he rejoined the private sector and become Vice President of Public Relations and Area Development at American Airlines.
- He served as Deputy Executive Director of the International Advertising Association.
- Barney joined The Rotary Club of New York in 1987. He held posts as Representative to the United Nations.
- At the UN, he served as Chair of The NGO Executive Committee, as a member of the NGO Committees on Sustainable Development and Population and Development.
- In a published interview entitled, Why Do We Need the UN? appearing in the July 2009 edition of The Rotarian magazine, Barney answered, "With all its faults, the UN is the only place in the world where it all comes together. Newspapers mainly report on the Security Council, so people don't realize that 80% of the UN's work is humanitarian. No other place has [so much] information and resources, and all these people coming together, including civil society (NGOs). That's got to be worth something."
- He and his wife of 68 years, DeeDee, travelled widely; they supported many charities and read regularly to the blind.
- Barney was active in Yale Alumni affairs all his life.
- He is survived by his two sons and three grandchildren.
- His wife, DeeDee, died in 2009.

EPILOGUE

Thanks to Mr. Sylvan Barnett and Dr. Josef Klee, who organized most of the conversations between Rotary and the UN upon which this book is based, I hope the information from these meetings provide the reader with a clearer understanding of the United Nations.

While the United Nations was initially created to defeat Japan and Germany during World War II, it must be pointed out at that time, Joseph Stalin, aka "Uncle Joe," was our ally. Pre-communist China was invited to join as one of the five Permanent Members of the Security Council, and then the Communist Revolution occurred two years later. Also, the UN's recognition of Israel as a Jewish State infuriated the Arab world. Yet, in spite of these "deal-breaking" epochal events, the UN did survive its early years!

After learning of its early history, it is difficult for me to imagine that the United Nations could have turned into such a massive, diverse organization. While the Security Council is still dealing with such issues as North Korea, Syria, and other regional conflicts, the reader should now have a better understanding of the countless poverty reduction, educational, human rights, and health programs. It should also be well-defined how the UN has also provided the platform for NGOs such as Rotary International to meet their humanities goals.

It does become obvious that these NGOs are the "boots on the ground" for many of the UN programs. It is also my sincere hope that this book has introduced you to the diverse personalities of the dedicated men and women trying to meet the lofty goals of the *Preamble of the United Nations Charter*.

There have been several major studies and commissions to help modernize and reform the United Nations with many chronic issues to be dealt with. For example, the "One China Policy," and why is France still a permanent member of the Security Council, yet not Japan and Germany? But the United Nations has survived, and there has not been a major war among the great-powers of the world since its founding.

EPILOGUE

The first line of the UN Charter Preamble says it all: "*We the peoples of the UNITED NATIONS determined to save succeeding generations from the scourge of war, which twice in our lifetime has brought untold sorrow to mankind.*"—and they have been determined!

WHAT IS THE ROTARY CLUB OF NEW YORK?

Established in 1909, The Rotary Club of New York provides Civic-minded business and professional men and women with an enjoyable and organized way to make a contribution to our city and to needy areas of the world. We meet weekly and plan club, community, and international service activities. By using our skills and expertise, members also enhance their professional network, career development, and cross-cultural understanding. All Rotary Clubs are nonreligious, nongovernmental, and open to every race, culture, and creed. Our membership represents a cross section of local civic-minded business and professional leaders.

THE NEW YORK ROTARY FOUNDATION supports more than two dozen organizations which have included the Salvation Army, YM-YWCA, Boy Scouts, Columbia Presbyterian Medical Center, Madison Square Boys and Girls Club, Saint Agnes Soup Kitchen, Horizon Concerts, National Association for Visually Handicapped, Police and Firemen's Recognition Day, and Polio Plus.

New York Rotary's "SERVICE ABOVE SELF" awards program honors members who excel in community work.

ACRONYMS AND ABBREVIATIONS

ACABQ—Administrative and Budgetary Questions

ACA—American Council on Africa

ADB—Asian Development Bank

AfDB—African Development Bank

AFISMA—African-led International Support Mission in Mali: replaced by MINUSMA (United Nations Multidimensional Integrated Stabilization Mission in Mali) ad interim; not usually written out

AIDS—Acquired immunodeficiency syndrome; not usually written out

APEC—Asia-Pacific Economic Cooperation

ASEAN—Association of Southeast Asian Nations

AWF—Asian Women's Fund

BONUCA. United Nations Peacebuilding Support Office in the Central African Republic: replaced by BINUCA (United Nations Integrated Peacebuilding Office in the Central African Republic)

CAR—Central African Republic

CARICOM—Caribbean Community

CCISUA—Coordinating Committee for International Staff Unions and Associations of the United Nations System

CEB—United Nations System Chief Executives Board for Coordination

CEDAW—Committee on the Elimination of Discrimination Against Women

CELAC—Community of Latin American and Caribbean States

CFCs—Chlorofluorocarbons

CIS—Commonwealth of Independent States

CONGO—Conference of NGOs

CPA—Coalition Provisional Authority

CPI—Consumer Price Index

CPN—Communist Party of Nepal later split into two groups in 1995 under the newly elected Prime Minister Deuba: CPN/M (Maoist) and CPN/UML (Unified Marxist Lenin)

CSD—Commission on Sustainable Development

CSW—Commission on the Status of Women: part of the United Nations ECOSOC (Economic and Social Council)

DDF—District Designated Fund

DESA—United Nations Department of Economic and Social Affairs

DNA—Deoxyribonucleic Acid; never written out

DPA—Department of Political Affairs

DPI—Department of Public Information

DSD—Division of Sustainable Development

EBRD—European Bank for Reconstruction and Development

ECA—Economic Commission for Africa

ECE—Economic Commission for Europe

ECOSOC—Economic and Social Council

EFTA—European Free Trade Association

ESCAP—Economic and Social Commission for Asia and the Pacific

ESCWA—Economic and Social Commission for Western Asia

EU—European Union

EUFOR—European Union Military Operation in Bosnia and Herzegovina

EUROPOL—European Police Office

EUROSTAT—European Union statistical office; never written out

FANCI—Forces Armées Nationales de Côte d'Ivoire

FAO—Food and Agriculture Organization of the United Nations

FDI—Foreign Direct Investment

FICSA—Federation of International Civil Servants' Associations

FNL—Forces Nationales de Libération (Burundi)

GATT—General Agreement on Tariffs and Trade

GOL—Gift of Life International, Rotarian-based organization

GDP—Gross Domestic Product

GEF—Global Environment Facility

GIS—Geographic Information System

GNP—Gross National Product

GPS—Global Positioning System

GSE—Government-sponsored Enterprise

GSP—Generalized System of Preferences

HDI—United Nations Human Development Index

H.E.—Abbreviation for His or Her Excellency

HIV—Human Immunodeficiency Virus; not usually written out

IADB—Inter-American Development Bank

IAEA—International Atomic Energy Agency

IASC—Inter-Agency Standing Committee

IANWGE—Inter-Agency Network on Women and Gender Equality

IBRD—International Bank for Reconstruction and Development

ICAO—International Civil Aviation Organization

ICC—International Christian Concern

ICFTU—International Confederation of Free Trade Unions

ICRC—International Committee of the Red Cross

ICSC—International Civil Service Commission

ICSU—International Council for Science (formerly International Council of Scientific Unions)

ICT—Information and Communications Technology

IDA—International Development Association

IDB—Islamic Development Bank

IFAD—International Fund for Agricultural Development

IFC—International Finance Corporation

IGAD—Intergovernmental Authority on Development

IIRR—International Institute of Rural Construction

ILO—International Labour Organization

IMF—International Monetary Fund—

IMIS—Integrated Management Information System

IMO—International Maritime Organization

INSTRAW—International Research and Training Institute for the Advancement of Women (transferred to UN Women)

INTERPOL—International Criminal Police Organization

IOM—International Organization for Migration

IP—Internet Protocol; not usually written out

IPSAS—International Public Sector Accounting Standards

IPU—Inter-Parliamentary Union

IPW—Iran Press Watch

ISAF—International Security Assistance Force (Afghanistan)

ITC—International Trade Centre

ITNs—Insecticide Treated Nets

ITU—International Telecommunication Union

JEM—Justice and Equality Movement (Sudan)

JPOI—Johannesburg Plan of Implementation

JVA—Juba Valley Alliance (Somalia)

KFOR—Kosovo Force

LAS—League of Arab States

LDCs—Least Developed Countries

LGN—Logos Global Network

LIFE—Literacy Initiative for Empowerment

MDGs—UN Millennium Development Goals

MFA—Ministry of Foreign Affairs

MINUSTAH—United Nations Stabilization Mission in Haiti

MTF—Maritime Task Force

NAFTA—the North American Free Trade Agreement

NATO—North Atlantic Treaty Organization

NEPAD—New Partnership for Africa's Development

NGO—Nongovernmental Organization

NPT—Nuclear Nonproliferation Treaty Review Conference

OAS—Organization of American States

OAU—Organization of African Unity (now African Union)

ODA—Official Development Assistance

ODS—Official Document System

OECD—Organization for Economic Cooperation and Development

OECS—Organisation of Eastern Caribbean States

OHCHR—Office of the United Nations High Commissioner for Human Rights

OIC—Organization of Islamic Cooperation (formerly Organization of the Islamic Conference)

OIF—International Organization of la Francophonie

OIP—Oil-for-Food Programme

OIOS—Office of Internal Oversight Services

ONUB—United Nations Operation in Burundi

OPCW—Organisation for the Prohibition of Chemical Weapons

OPEC—Organization of the Petroleum Exporting Countries

OSAGI—Office of Special Advisor on Gender Issues and the Advancement of Women

OSCE—Organization for Security and Cooperation in Europe

PAHO—Pan American Health Organization

PLO—Palestine Liberation Organization

POLISARIO— Frente Polisario Frente Popular para la Liberación de Saguía el-Hamra y de Río de Oro (Western Sahara)

PPAF—The Public-Private Alliance Foundation

PPP—Purchasing Power Parity: a theory which states that exchange rates between currencies are in equilibrium when their purchasing power is the same in each of the two countries.

PRC—People's Republic of China – Mainland China

RI—Rotary International

RNA—Ribonucleic Acid; never written out

ROC—Republic of China (Taiwan)

ROR—Reach Out and Read

SAARC—South Asian Association for Regional Cooperation

TAL—Transitional Administrative Law

TRF—The Rotary Foundation

TRIPS—Trade-Related Intellectual Property Rights

UHF—Ultra High Frequency; not usually written out

UNAIDS—Joint United Nations Programme on HIV/AIDS

UNAMI—United Nations Assistance Mission for Iraq

UNAMSIL—United Nations Mission in Sierra Leone

UNCDF—United Nations Capital Development Fund

UNCITRAL—United Nations Commission on International Trade Law

UNCTAD—United Nations Conference on Trade and Development

UNDAW—UN Division for the Advancement of Women

UNDOF—United Nations Disengagement Observer Force (Golan Heights)

UNDP—United Nations Development Programme

UNDPI—United Nations Department of Information

UNEP—United Nations Environment Programme

UNESCO—United Nations Educational, Scientific and Cultural Organization

UNFICYP—United Nations Peacekeeping Force in Cyprus

UNFIP—United Nations Fund for International Partnerships

UNFPA—United Nations Population Fund

UN-Habitat—United Nations Human Settlements Programme

UNHCR—Office of the United Nations High Commissioner for Refugees

UNICEF—United Nations International Children's Emergency Fund or better known as United Nations Children's Fund

UNIDIR—United Nations Institute for Disarmament Research

UNIDO—United Nations Industrial Development Organization

UNIFEM—United Nations Development Fund for Women: transferred to UN Women

UNIFIL—United Nations Interim Force in Lebanon

UNITAR—United Nations Institute for Training and Research

UNMOGIP—United Nations Military Observer Group in India and Pakistan

UNMOVIC—United Nations Monitoring, Verification and Inspection Commission (Iraq)

UNO—United Nations Organization

UNOCA—United Nations Regional Office for Central Africa

UNOCI—United Nations Operation in Côte d'Ivoire

UNODC—United Nations Office on Drugs and Crime

UNOPS—United Nations Office for Project Services

UNRRA—United Nations Relief and Rehabilitation Administration

UNTSO—United Nations Truce Supervision Organization (Middle East)

UNU—United Nations University

UNV—United Nations Volunteers Programme

UN Women—United Nations Entity for Gender Equality and the Empowerment of Women

UNWTO—World Tourism Organization

UPU—Universal Postal Union

USCIRF—United States Commission on International Religious Freedom

USAID—United States Agency for International Development

USDA—United States Department of Agriculture

USFMEP—US Federation for Middle East Peace

UT, UTC—Universal Time, Universal Time Coordinated; not usually written out

VAT—Value Added Tax

VHF—Very High Frequency; not usually written out

WAEMU—West African Economic and Monetary Union

WASH—Water, Sanitation, and Hygiene program

WEOG—Western Europe and Others Group

WFP—World Food Programme

WHO—World Health Organization

WIDER—World Institute for Development Economics Research

WIPO—World Intellectual Property Organization

WMD—Weapons of Mass Destruction

WMO—World Meteorological Organization

WSSD—World Summit on Sustainable Development

WTO—World Trade Organization

CONTRIBUTORS

Josef Klee, PhD is a member of the Bal Harbour Rotary Club. He was a member of the New York Rotary Club from 1977 to 2014, where for twelve years, he organized the International Breakfast Meetings at the United Nations with Ambassadors and Senior UN Officials as speakers addressing political, economic, human rights issues, and other global topics.

For twenty years, he served as a manager in different offices of the UN Secretariat in New York. After his retirement, and until today, he has been an advisor to the Holy See Mission and teaches as an adjunct professor at the Seaton Hall School of Diplomacy and at the Law School of St. Thomas University in Miami. He has published several books and numerous articles about management topics and UN-related issues.

Sheila Washington is a Wall Street Rotarian from the Rotary Club of New York formerly from San Diego, California. She faithfully travelled into Manhattan from Brooklyn, NY to attend monthly International Breakfast Meetings when the author could not be present. She always made meetings ever more interesting, as she would carefully write up a review of meeting conversations, which we are pleased to be able to include in this book.

For more information regarding
Thomas V. McConnon and his work,
Email Tom at thomasrefny@gmail.com

Additional copies of this book may be purchased online from
www.LegworkTeam.com; www.Amazon.com;
or www.BarnesandNoble.com

You can also obtain a copy of the book by
ordering it from your favorite bookstore.

ABOUT THE AUTHOR

Thomas V. McConnon, has been a longtime supporter and active member of Rotary International since starting up a technical training program as a Peace Corps Volunteer in the early 1980s in partnership with The Rotary Foundation and the United States Agency for international Development.

Before joining the Peace Corps, Tom was a financial analyst at Dun and Bradstreet in New York, and editor and manager of their publication *Key Business Ratios*. Previous to joining Dun and Bradstreet, he was a research assistant to the staff economists at Townsend-Greenspan & Company, the former Chairman of the Federal Reserve of the United States, Alan Greenspan's economic forecasting company.

Tom is currently the CEO of Thomas Refrigeration, Inc., a leading company in its field that provides mechanical services primarily to New York City area real estate managers and owners. Since 2004, Tom has assisted in conducting the Rotary Club of New York's monthly International Breakfast Meetings and was editor and contributor for "Inside the United Nations Blog", and a frequent contributor to Rotary International Day at the United Nations review.

He lives on Long Island, New York with his wife Noemi, whom he met while serving with the Peace Corps, and somehow was lucky enough to convince her to move to the United States. They have five children, and seven grandchildren at the printing of this book, and God Willing, are looking forward to several more.

Tom earned a BS Degree in Economics from New York University in the late 1970s and completed his MBA Degree shortly after returning from the Peace Corps. *(He was about seventy-five percent through before joining the Peace Corps)*

CPSIA information can be obtained
at www.ICGtesting.com
Printed in the USA
BVHW03*1719150318
510321BV00001B/1/P